IAN
RANKIN AND
INSPECTOR
REBUS

IAN
RANKIN AND
INSPECTOR
REBUS

Craig Cabell

metro

Published by John Blake Publishing Ltd,
3 Bramber Court, 2 Bramber Road,
London W14 9PB, England

www.johnblakepublishing.co.uk

First published in hardback in 2010
This edition 2011

ISBN: 978 1 84358 292 2

British Library Cataloguing-in-Publication Data:

A catalogue record for this book is available from the British Library.

Design by www.envydesign.co.uk

Printed in Great Britain by CPI Bookmarque, Croydon CR0 4TD

1 3 5 7 9 10 8 6 4 2

Papers used by John Blake Publishing are natural, recyclable products made from
wood grown in sustainable forests. The manufacturing processes conform to the
environmental regulations of the country of origin.

For Doreen Porter, Tracey Allen, Mark Ottowell, David Barlow and Graham A Thomas – professional editors, journalists and pure artists all. My thanks and best wishes for the friendship and time we spent together on *Focus*.

Also, to the great writers and editors of Scotland – past and present.

'"I'm not supposed to be here," Detective Inspector John Rebus said. Not that anyone was listening.'

Fleshmarket Close

'It was all Sherlock Holmes' fault, really.'

Ian Rankin Presents Criminal Minded

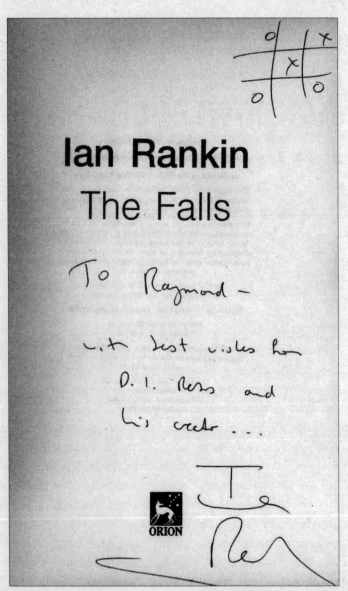

Ian Rankin
The Falls

To Raymond –

with best wishes from
D. I. Ross and
his creator ...

A copy of *The Falls* signed by Ian Rankin… and Inspector Rebus.

ACKNOWLEDGEMENTS

First I would like to thank Ian Rankin himself, for the many interviews and other conversations/emails over the years (including that alfresco breakfast meeting in the heart of winter!), Helen Richardson at Orion for always being so generous and accommodating, Tricia Malley and Ross Gillespie for their kindness and assistance with photographs (lovely people), Ellie Graham at Titan, Campbell Armstrong, John Connolly, Frederick Forsyth, James Herbert, Bernard Cornwall, for being great friends and mentors over the years, also Michael Connolly, Jeffrey Deaver, Peter James, the late great Ed McBain, for their time; and the spirits of Spark, Hogg, Stevenson, Conan Doyle, Burns and Scott, who continue to play their part in our lives.

CRAIG CABELL

Also thanks to Anita, Samantha, Nathan, Fern, who have to put up with my thought processes on a daily basis and — in regard to Nathan — treading the Edinburgh streets in search of Rebus's Scotland too. Thanks also to legendary cops Leonard 'Nipper' Reed and Peter Wilton, who gave me a strong insight into the Police Forces of the UK over the past 50-odd years; and Lenny Hamilton, Billy Frost, Charlie Kray, Ronnie Knight and the Dixon brothers who have given me their perceptions about the criminal underworld. Thanks also to Everington, Evans-Hendrick, Savage, Felton, Holdcroft, Fletcher, Townsend and Cherry, in fact all at the BTK, who have been my spiritual backbone over the past four years regarding internal security and other relevant areas of expertise. Thanks are also due to Euan and Iris Martyn; Euan has been a good friend over the years from north of the border with a keen perception and wit, especially when I've had to pull rank! Thanks also to Tony Mulliken for being Tony Mulliken and reminding me that you can still do six impossible things before — or during! — breakfast (Miami Rules or not!). Thanks also to Samantha Hammell for helping me solve Edinburgh's secret of Sherlock Holmes, a shame our conversation was cut short but so was the queue! Thanks to Doreen and Tracey, Mark, Dave and GT for being such a great team: you all kept me sane during the early years (long live Office 2). Thanks also to the genius of David Bowie, Bruce Springsteen, Pink Floyd, Lou Reed, Bob Dylan, John Lennon and The Beatles and, of course, The Rolling Stones, for the musical accompaniment while I proofed the book (a bit of method-writing at the end there!). Finally, thanks also to my father who found ten early Stones' albums for me and additionally keeps my children covered in artist's paints and glues on a regular basis when I have to work — perhaps we should invite you over for bath time soon!

Sincerely, many thanks to all.

Craig Cabell
Blackheath, August 2009

CONTENTS

PREFACE

'But it wasn't all image, was it?'

Ian Rankin, *Strip Jack*

Ian Rankin and Inspector Rebus. There's a coincidence in that title: the first letter of each name is the same – IR. Okay, Rebus's first name is John not Inspector; but the analogy endures, especially when we acknowledge that the only description we get of Rebus in the first novel is that he has brown hair and green eyes – the same as his creator Ian Rankin.

So Rankin created something of a self-image in Rebus? An interesting question and one that can't be answered in a simple preface.

This is not a biography of Ian Rankin and it is not an in-depth piece of literary criticism. It's somewhere between the two, that interesting place, which is part fact and part fiction, the area where Ian Rankin encounters Inspector John Rebus and the character and stories take shape.

I decided to write this book after reading – and listening to – Rankin's entertaining *Rebus's Scotland*, a book – or audio if you prefer it – in which Rankin seeks answers to complicated questions such as: What is Edinburgh? And, am I indeed John Rebus?

As a Scot he probably answered the first question successfully through a range of observations and experiences, although perhaps leaving himself open to a slight charge of xenophobia along the way; but perhaps that's where you'll find John Rebus – or where Rankin wants you to find him?

I personally felt that Rankin was too close to himself (and Rebus) to answer the second question in *Rebus's Scotland*. So what you have here is my version of the answer to the important question, is Rankin, Rebus? Or, based on the assumption that every character is based on the writer who created it: how much of Rankin is Rebus?

Throughout this book you will learn all that a reader really needs to know about an author: the path of his life up to becoming a writer, his thought processes connected with the formation of his main character and his adopted city, and how the main characters in the novels have developed over the years. You will also see how Rankin's style has developed over the years too, becoming more intricate.

The things you won't find here are in-depth discussions about police procedure, social and economic issues raised by the plotlines, and analysis of inconsistencies throughout the books, which are all part of the wider picture of literary criticism. I'm simply interested in the man and his creation here and the parallels between them.

That said, what you will find here are basic plotlines for every Rebus novel (without giving away the punchlines), character analysis, extensive interviews with Ian Rankin over a ten-year period, a TV guide and a detailed bibliography and collector's guide. The end product is a solid companion work to Ian Rankin and John Rebus. And if that is not enough, there is an uncut interview with Rankin in Rebus's watering hole, the Oxford Bar, by way of conclusion.

OK, so that's the sales pitch over with: what about those questions I wanted to answer? Well, let us now walk the atmospheric streets of Rankin's – Rebus's – Edinburgh and seek the answers together...

> 'Rebus was still trying to come to terms with his new workplace. Everything was so tidy, he could never find anything, as a result of which he was always keen to get out of the office and onto the street.'
>
> *The Black Book*

NOTE ON
THE TEXT

I have deliberately spelled out the titles of Ian Rankin's novels in full throughout this book: *Knots and Crosses*, *Hide and Seek*, *Tooth and Nail*, rather than using ampersand, which is inconsistently used throughout Rankin's published work.

With regard to *Tooth and Nail*, I use its original title *Wolfman* up to the point where the change of title was accepted by Rankin (after being suggested by his American publisher).

I call Robert Louis Stevenson's novella *Strange Case of Dr Jekyll and Mr Hyde*, the exact title it was published under in January 1886. I only adapt an abbreviated version of the title when the flow of the text dictates it.

All quotes are credited in footnotes. However, for the early interviews that support the facts of the author's early life, I leave these unrecorded as I rarely quote Rankin directly in the text (basically my *Set in Darkness* interview); other interviews are fully credited.

I have used several sound bites from other journalists/publications, which are fully credited in the text and/or in End Notes, although these are few.

Craig Cabell
The Pleasance, Eltham, August 2009

CHAPTER ONE

GIMME SHELTER

'Here's the scoop: crime writing is sexy.'

Ian Rankin presents Criminal Minded

Ian Rankin was born in Cardenden, Fife, on 28 April 1960, 'a rough working class town', he explains.[i] Cardenden is situated in central Fife, between Kirkcaldy and Dunfermline, and sprang up in Victorian times with the growth of the coal-mining industry. Today, the mines are closed and unemployment is endemic.

Rankin's home was 17 Craigmead Terrace, a small house his parents lived in from the time it was built in 1960 – shortly after Rankin was born – until his father's untimely death in 1990.

Rankin's parents got together through tragic circumstances. His father had been married before and his

---

i Author interview 14 January 2002.

wife had died; his mother had been married before and her husband had died. So they met as widow and widower. Rankin would state that, 'Death was the reason they got together and had me... There has always been the shadow of death in my family.' Interesting thing to say and may explain book titles such as *Mortal Causes, The Naming of the Dead, Dead Souls, Let It Bleed, Death Comes at the End* (well, he has used the odd song title too!). Rankin's mother was a school dinner lady but sadly died when he was only 18. 'She died when she was only in her early fifties. They said it was a stroke and then MS, although eventually they called it lung cancer.'[ii]

This proved to be a very difficult time for Rankin and may explain his deep-rooted interest in the plight of people of all classes and how they struggle against incredible odds; it's a constant theme in his books.

His father died at the age of 72, an age Rankin doesn't consider to be that old. He was a dock worker, so Rankin grew up in a strong working-class environment, with two half-sisters as a legacy from his parents' previous marriages.

He went to school at Auchterderran Junior High for a couple of years and then Beath High School in Cowdenbeath, the latter being a four-mile bus ride from his home. Rankin gives a gritty picture of his formative years: 'The job opportunities in Fife during the 1960s and '70s were not diverse. You would either go into the Armed

---

ii From 'The Tracks of my Years' by Andrew Preston, *Night & Day*, Association Newspapers, 24 October 2004.

Forces or the Police Force. That was pretty much it. People would get to the age of 16 or 18 and just leave and you'd never see them again.'[iii]. Not surprising then that the fictional John Rebus did both (Armed Forces and Police Force), as he was also born in Cardenden and in the same cul-de-sac as Rankin! But what about Rankin himself? Did he feel that these careers were the only options open to him? Perhaps to begin with he did; but he wanted something different and, not unlike the proverbial fairytale, he escaped and achieved it. He went on to higher education and broke the mould for Cardenden and his own family, who had never pursued further education.

In the light of all this, we could argue that through Rebus, Rankin has written about his breathtaking escape from the normal career path of a lad from Cardenden.

This isn't completely true but there are some strong parallels between the author and his creation.

Rankin would say that he started his literary life as a short story writer – well, a comic book writer to be brutal.[iv]

At the ages of six, seven and eight, he would draw stick-men cartoons with speech bubble stories, folding sheets of plain paper to form little booklets with typical boy-themes such as football, war and space.[v] This went on for

---

iii Author interview 14 January 2002.

iv See Introduction to *Beggars Banquet* and segment that forms the introduction to *The Scotsman Exclusive Souvenir Paperback Celebrating 20 Years of Inspector Rebus*.

v A very interesting pastime for die-hard Rankin fans, is spotting *Dr Who*/SF references throughout Ian's work (several times at least, see *Black and Blue*, special intro to *Knots and Crosses* and others).

several years until it was pointed out to him that he couldn't draw!

At the age of 10 or 11 he started to listen to music, but his 'obsessive' (his word not mine) behaviour meant that it wasn't good enough just to listen to the music, he wanted to form a band too. His friends weren't interested but he decided to write song lyrics and form a band in his head called The Amoebas.

This vivid fantasy world may give the general reader the impression that Rankin was a stay-at-home goody-goody but he wasn't. He had tough friends while growing up and he eventually did his own bit of thuggery with them, including shoplifting and fighting.[vi] Reading became Rankin's escape and was probably his saviour too. It certainly gave him a broader outlook academically, because if one reads at a young age then one tends to want to write, and the writing bug separated Rankin from his friends: 'I grew up feeling "different" from my family and friends, and trying desperately to blend in.' He said this in an almost throw-away sentence towards the end of *Rebus's Scotland* and said something similar to artist Jack Vettriano: 'I did like my own company. I felt very different. I felt like a chameleon. I was trying to look like I fitted in but I didn't really fit in… from an early age I felt they wouldn't understand because what I was doing was so out [of touch] with the tribe I was with; I was this dude who wanted to write poetry and short stories.'[vii]

---

vi See *Rebus's Scotland – A Personal Guide* (Orion, 2005).

vii *Artworks Scotland – When Ian Rankin met Jack Vettriano* (2009).

IAN RANKIN AND INSPECTOR REBUS

Writing certainly separated Rankin from his street-corner pals and family while growing up, and that distance formed the central theme of isolation – albeit in a more extreme way – in his first attempt at a novel, as he explained: 'My first novel was only about 40 pages long but it was about a teenager whose parents didn't understand him so he ran away to London... there was a lot of autobiography in that. I probably wanted to run away to London but I didn't have the gumption to do it. I always kept that side of [my personality] hidden away.'[viii]

It is very easy to blow this part of Rankin's life out of proportion. He didn't alienate himself; he simply became a little secretive in order to protect his hobby. I once asked him about his early friendships in juxtaposition to his growing interest in reading: 'I used to hang around street corners and there would be great affiliation between the guys and we would fight other youths in the towns nearby. We would pass around books like *Skinhead* and *Suedehead*, lots of pulp fiction.' So his friends did read; but Rankin took it one step further when he couldn't get into the cinema to see the films that were an extension of the pulp fiction he passed around his cronies: 'Suddenly along came *A Clockwork Orange*. I wasn't old enough to go and see it at the flicks; I was only 11 or 12 when it was released, so I went to the library and got it out. I couldn't believe that the librarian would let me do that. And the same thing happened with *The Godfather*. Nobody said to me, "Hey, are you 18?" And I suddenly found that there was no

viii *Artworks Scotland – When Ian Rankin met Jack Vettriano* (2009).

censorship with books. And therefore I started reading voraciously. I started reading the books of the films I couldn't get in to see. And my parents were so thrilled! They didn't care what I was reading as long as I was reading and not watching the television.'[ix]

Here lies the rub. Rankin wasn't pressured into reading: he chose to read in order to get at the stories he couldn't see at the cinema. Couple this with his imagination and general interest in books/comics, a strong hobby started to evolve in his life.

We have already found that Rankin didn't feel that he fitted in too well with his friends, he also didn't want to stay in Cardenden all his life and become a serviceman or policeman, he wanted to break away from all of that, as he qualified to Jack Vettriano: '… how I started to write books… replace the real drab Fife of the '60s with an alternative universe.' This 'feel-good' world he created for himself, the security blanket of escape, accidentally made him a self-starter in the academic world. It gave him a perspective about books and therefore a grounding that took him further along the educational path and yes, he can thank himself for that; with some quality English teachers along the way (who almost act like spiritual guides throughout his formative years).

On that basis it is perhaps no surprise that in the last year of High School Rankin was sent back to his Primary School, Denend, to follow the daily life of a teacher, as the noble profession seemed to be his obvious calling!

---

ix Author interview 14 January 2002.

He didn't enjoy the experience too much, but something inspirational did happen to him in the classroom while there and kindled the flame of an academic profession: he became aware of a nationwide poetry competition.

It is said that writers are born, not made, and it is clear that this strain of creative pursuit was embedded in Rankin from a very early age and endured throughout his character-building formative years. It then evolved with his maturity and keen perception in his teens. He must have had a driving passion for writing to do something that nobody else in his family circle had done, nor indeed his friends. But he *was* driven and therefore determined to make the best of his skills. And it eventually paid off too.

His first stab at a poetry competition won him second prize. The poem was called *Euthanasia*, a dark subject to say the least. He was 17. He didn't publicise his success to his friends and family. He kept his hobby secret, an unrequited love affair, which he knew would be vehemently rejected by his friends, as he explains: 'Growing up in a rough mining town I couldn't say to my friends that I sat in my room writing poetry, song lyrics for non-existent bands and short stories. They would have smacked me in the mouth and called me a poof.'[x]

Rankin could have kept the whole thing a secret if he hadn't been so successful! Suddenly he won both a poetry competition and a short story competition and found himself mentioned in the local newspapers, where he finally had to admit his secret passion for words. It was a

x Author interview 14 January 2002.

shock to both friends and family alike. However, this small-minded mentality wasn't shared by his English teacher, Mr Gillespie, who recognised his writing talents and encouraged him. Rankin pushed on, writing a story set in his own school, where a poster of Mick Jagger took on satanic powers and sent the children on a blood-curdling rampage (something he would later admit had more than a passing influence from *Lord of the Flies*). So Ian Rankin was a horror writer? Well, no, but the darkness in life has always interested him and, let us remind ourselves of the title of that award-winning poem, *Euthanasia*, and appreciate that death is not the end for Ian Rankin; it's simply the part where the analysis of the dead by the living begins!

It was partially Mr Gillespie's encouragement that inspired Rankin to go on to higher education. This was where tutors and academics began to advise him to great effect, a process that seemed to shape his literary growth throughout his education, especially at university, where there were more older, wiser teachers and writers to guide him.

Rankin always listened to the older literary voice (even those ghosts that whispered from bookshelves) and it stood him in good stead too. This isn't a new concept: authors such as Campbell Armstrong, James Herbert and Clive Barker experienced similar support; and it's good to see young talent being spotted by teachers at all levels, people who can detect the shining diamonds. It doesn't have to be subjects like English or art – sport and the sciences have their child stars too.

IAN RANKIN AND INSPECTOR REBUS

So Ian Rankin went to university at the age of 18 and pursued a literary career? Not quite. New Wave beckoned first! Around 1979/80 (aged 19/20) Rankin became a member of a punk rock band: 'I have always liked music but never had the patience – or skill – to learn an instrument. I used my poetry as song lyrics. We recorded five songs for a demo tape, but got nowhere. We only played six or seven times.'[xi]

Music is a constant in Rankin's books and it seems logical that he would try his hand along the way. In fact, quite recently, Rankin has teamed up with Aidan Moffat and St Jude's Infirmary to write songs and he has also toured with Jackie Leven – albeit reciting a short story, not contributing song lyrics![xii] He's also a self-confessed vinyl junkie, who constantly scans the record shops for more obscure albums to satiate his eclectic tastes.

His love of music and books settled him down to university life, but it was here that his personal life took a serious knock-back: his mother fell gravely ill. Her slow death made things very challenging for the young man, as he explained in a very tender interview with Andrew Preston for *Night & Day*: 'I was busy as a student during the week and then going home on a Friday night to see my mum. It was a terrible situation because I hated to go home and see her slowly deteriorate. One day I was sitting on her bed and she said she wished she was dead. How do you respond to that?'

---

xi Author interview 26 July 2009.

xii See Rankin/Leven's CD *Jackie Leven Said*.

Simply, Rankin responded by working his socks off and giving his mother – or her lasting memory – something to be proud of.[xiii] He no longer had to be a closet academic: he was with like-minded people at university and his future path was clear. 'When I went to university in Edinburgh it became a great release. Suddenly there were groups of people writing. I went to pubs and I'd see a famous poet.' This thrilled the young man and inspired him to travel onwards; however, he did become slightly despondent at the lack of novelists in Edinburgh, as he stated: 'There were not so many famous novelists in Edinburgh, which was a little frustrating for me. There were some in Glasgow but not Edinburgh.'[xiv]

This is a very important point. The urge to be a novelist was there as soon as he went to university and he was frustrated that having 'come out' as a writer, he didn't find any kindred spirits. There were other people writing and talking about books but no fellow would-be novelists. So he found one – a hero – somebody to emulate, focus on, aspire to. 'William McIlvanney was my great influence. He wrote three crime novels but he was a

---

xiii For a concert at Queen's Hall, Edinburgh, in August 2004, Rankin read a short (non-Rebus) story about a young man made good, who returns to his home in Fife to attend the funeral of his mother. Although *Jackie Leven Said* is not exactly autobiographical, it has tiny fragments of autobiography mixed in with the fiction, such as being allowed to sneak into the cinema under age even though the ticker seller was a neighbour and knew he was under age. But there is a more important point: the isolation of the main character amongst his own kin. This seems to mirror Rankin's own feelings of his formative years [*Jackie Leven Says – Jackie Leven and Ian Rankin*, Cooking Vinyl 2005].

xiv Author interview 14 January 2002.

serious literary writer. He had won the Whitbread Prize and I thought, If it's good enough for him then it's good enough for me.'[xv]

Again, Rankin's single-minded determination is clear. Already we are talking crime fiction here and he finds an academic crime writer to have as a major influence, to justify his passion for his chosen pursuit. No surprise then that he would study English Literature and English Language at Edinburgh University. All the eggs were going into one basket and his passion paid off when he graduated in 1982.

It wasn't all plain sailing from then on. It may look easy when laid down in a book where we all know the final outcome, but that period was tough for Rankin – not just the death of his mother and his studies, but the lack of money and the Edinburgh cold too. In his book *Rebus's Scotland*, he described the bitter mornings where he walked into the freezing Edinburgh wind to attend lectures and lessons. Initially he lived a 15-minute walk away at Marchmont; but the student life is a maverick one at the best of times and he moved around a lot from there.

Having little money and living in small flats gives students perception and independence and Rankin found time to think more about his hobby of writing. He moved into Edinburgh's New Town, but the weather was still miserable and he still needed to walk up the big hill into the Old Town to attend lectures every day.

---

xv Author interview 14 January 2002.

'... that bitter and biting wind which whipped across the streets of Edinburgh in summer as well as winter.'

Wolfman

These early years left a vivid impression on the young man. When, much later, a novelist and living in the relative warmth of the south of France (for six years), Rankin could still summon vivid images of Edinburgh's tough winters: they were ingrained in his mind. They were strong memories of his university days, of walking the characteristic streets, and those streets forged the writer we know today: a man passionate about location and that location is quite often – but not always – Edinburgh, his spiritual home, the place that shaped him into the person he was destined to be, a best-selling novelist. It was a place where he truly came of age or, more accurately, fulfilled his potential; a place he calls his hometown nowadays – and that is important to understand. Rankin will always tell you that he is from the Kingdom of Fife but his hometown is Edinburgh, the home of many of Scotland's literary greats. And he takes great comfort from their spiritual presence.

'Rebus turned and found himself confronting a statue of Sir Walter Scott... Scott looked as though he'd heard every word but wasn't about to pass judgement.

"Keep it that way," Rebus warned, not caring who might hear.'

Mortal Causes

Between 1983 and 1986 Rankin worked on a PhD thesis on the work of Muriel Spark. It was at this point that he became heavily involved in his own writing, which did cause him some concern. 'I'd gone through university, done my MA in American Literature, a PhD on the novels of Muriel Spark and I was going to be an academic. I was sitting in a library all day poring over books. And to write a crime novel was a bit of a problem in as much as it was working below the level I was currently working at. How could I go to university professors and say, "I write crime novels"? I thought they'd just laugh at me. But when William McIlvanney did it, I suddenly thought that it was OK to do it.'[xvi]

Yes, Rankin did question his dream but again found a kindred spirit in an older, wiser academic, not just his favourite author. 'There was a writer in residence. A lovely guy called Allan Massie, who was a serious novelist and I would take things along for him to look at. I told him that I thought I should be writing for my peers but I found that I was writing for a bigger audience. He agreed with me, saying that I may not get the kudos but I'd certainly get the cash!'[xvii]

So Rankin quickly learned that it was important to get paid and make a living. This is an important point because without money coming in after his academic studies, his dream would fail. The practicalities of life were merged with his dream of literary pursuit and fitted well; it justified

---

xvi Author interview 14 January 2002.

xvii Author interview 14 January 2002.

becoming a crime writer. This explains why Rankin had a series of different jobs after university. They were there to pay for his literary dream, even when he started writing the Rebus series – indeed he worked as a grape-picker and swineherd during his six years in France – but before then he was an alcohol researcher, taxman, college secretary. He was also a Literature tutor at the University of Edinburgh, where he retains an involvement with the James Tait Black Memorial Prize to this day.

When Rankin talks about these episodes in his life, they are always light-hearted. For example, alcohol researcher? Well, not so strange perhaps: this was a serious academic study. 'Being an alcohol researcher was the closest I ever became to being a private eye! It was a study at Edinburgh University and they got these 13-year-olds and questioned them on their drinking habits. Three years later, they went back to interview the kids again to see how they had changed. And I was on the second stage of this. I was given a list of names and addresses and I couldn't find these folk. So I had to track them down, get them on their own, without their parents around, so I could get some decent answers out of them. And I would be asking the same set of questions as they were asked previously. I got paid for each one.'[xviii]

So the job of alcohol researcher was a very serious one; Rankin wasn't just sitting in a pub drinking. But what did he find out from the study? 'I think what we ultimately found out was that 13-year-olds lie an awful lot about how much

---

xviii Author interview 14 January 2002.

they drink! I could see it in their eyes when I asked them, "How much did you drink last night?" The answer would be, "Oh, 15, maybe 16 pints." So then I would ask them how much money they took out with them, to which the answer was invariably about five quid!'[xix]

It was his experiences in and around the end of his university days that helped him with his Rebus series. The thought of Rankin sitting down with a 16-year-old lad questioning him on his drinking habits of the night before is so typically Rebus in pursuit of evidence to solve a major crime. That said, his brief experiences with adolescent drinking habits, intermixed with the antics of his own group of friends growing up in Cardenden, could have given him the grounding for a career as a social worker, but then again, some policemen feel like glorified social workers anyway!

> 'People say the Krays had a deprived upbringing and that this could have been what turned them to crime, but I reckon there was more money coming into their house than into ours.'
>
> *The Man Who Nicked the Krays* Nipper Read

Let us analyse all of this information for a moment, substituting Rankin for Rebus. Let's see how much of Rankin was Rebus before the detective was even a twinkle in his creator's eye. There's the tough Fife upbringing, the street-wise perception and the promise that physically he

---

could handle himself. Then there is the independence and training that university life would offer Rankin – that would be the Armed Forces and Police Force for Rebus. And the questioning of youths on their drinking habits? That's the social conscience of both Rebus and Rankin going to work; although Rebus would incur greater attitude in the 'interview room' than Rankin, especially as he got older!

The worldly wise aspect for Rankin was developed quite young. He had even experienced the death of a parent.

So we know what formed the writer and we appreciate where death touched his own life; but what brought all these threads together and created Rebus?

It wasn't a person. It was a city: Edinburgh, that cradle of Scottish fiction.

> "Twas grace that taught my heart to fear,
> And grace my fears relieved.'
>
> *Amazing Grace*

CHAPTER TWO

EDINBURGH, A TOWN CALLED JEKYLL AND HYDE

Craig Cabell: Sum up Edinburgh in one word?
Ian Rankin: Villagey.
Author interview, 26 July 2009

Some tourists emerge from Waverley station, deep in the heart of Edinburgh, and catch their breath: the ancient castle perched on the rocky hillside, the distinctive architecture of the tall buildings amidst the glitzy new shops on Princes Street, the sound of bagpipes emanating from the busy thoroughfare... These immediate images are strong, forceful, thrilling and fulfil the expectation of the average tourist, but there are other people who emerge from the station and see nothing but derelict souls in the dark, washed-out facades of the old buildings and ominous shadows slumbering beside the high-street shops.

'... the castle balanced solidly atop... crenellated building bricks. The orange street

17

lamps are crumpled toffee-wrappers glued to lollipop sticks.'

Dead Souls

Waverley station and Princes Street Gardens are the central locations that separate the Old Town of Edinburgh from the New Town and, the power of looking left at one thing and then right at another is a spectacle that leaves an indelible impression on many a tourist. The old and the new, the dark and the light, the Jekyll and Hyde; Edinburgh very quickly works its dark magic on the impressionable and is conjured in my mind by a passage from Robert Louis Stevenson's *The Slaying of Támanteá*: 'For fear inhabits the palace and grudging grows in the land.' There's almost a tangible fear embedded in Edinburgh's ancient countenance. It's conjured by the antique architecture of the city against the backdrop of the older – unspoilt – hinterland. That's the 'grudging' Stevenson alludes to, as if the preservation of such things allows these ancient emotions to linger – fester – for the sensitive to receive if they dare. Stevenson warns us in the same poem: 'And woe to him that comes short, and woe to him that delayed!'

Not everyone will detect the power of the yin and yang of Edinburgh: it's something that falls to a certain type of person with a certain turn of imagination. For hundreds of years Scottish writers have been writing about it and perhaps it's to them that Edinburgh offers the most intrigue and spectacle. Some may argue that Stevenson's poem has nothing to do with Edinburgh, but I see much of Stevenson discussing his hometown in the broader canvas of his work than he is given credit for. (Even though *Strange Case of Dr Jekyll and Mr Hyde* is set in London, it is about Edinburgh...)

> 'But I had other matters on my hand more pressing. Here I was in this old, black city, which was for all the world like a rabbit-warren, not only by the number of its indwellers, but the complication of its passages and holes. It was indeed a place where no stranger had a chance to find a friend, let be another stranger. Suppose him even to hit on the right close, people dwelt so thronged in these tall houses, he might very well seek a day before he chanced on the right door.'
>
> Robert Louis Stevenson, *Catriona*

Not all writers are as harsh as Stevenson. Muriel Spark sums up the city's cry for help in one poignant sentence:

> 'Sandy was bored, it did not seem necessary that the world should be saved, only that the poor people in the streets and slums of Edinburgh should be relieved.'
>
> *The Prime of Miss Jean Brodie*

From the ancient writer to the most modern, these men and women have tried to lay open the heart of Edinburgh, to get under its skin, to touch its soul, to understand it, to unlock its secrets and let the ancient corruptions pour out. For example, Edinburgh Castle, an active garrison to this day, has a dark, murky past, full of bloodshed and dark adventure, but it's also a catalyst for pride, patriotism and the perceived euphoria we all get from Robert Burns' *Auld Lang Syne*. Edinburgh, in that respect, is a mass of contradictions, as dark and ominous as the ancient passageways in both the Old and the New Towns.

Some people do not choose to see beneath the veneer of the city. They shy away from the little dark alleys that are nothing but slits split between buildings. They pull children along, travelling by main road only, and choose only that highway for the rest of their lives. But the washed-out recesses are rich pockets of possibility for a writer – and criminal! – where something sinister *must* have happened in the distant past or will happen very soon! Edinburgh provokes those with a dark imagination, as Rankin enthuses: 'There were no Ripper murders in Edinburgh… plenty of other grim stuff was happening though!'[xx] He almost says this with glee, overwhelmed by the myriad possibilities for his Edinburgh-based crime fiction.

Scotland has bred incredible literary giants: Burns, Scott, Stevenson, Conan Doyle, all of whom cut a nook out of the ancient city stone and spoke their minds of its influence. But one doesn't have to travel back to Victorian times to feel the presence of great literary influence. Contemporary writers such as Muriel Spark and Ian Rankin have carved a devilish niche in the ancient castle cliff-side all of their own. One astute reviewer mentioned that Rankin had not endeared himself to the Scottish Tourist Board after his first few Inspector Rebus novels, and that is probably quite true,

xx Author interview 26 July 2009.

because Rankin is a very keen observer of the darkness that slumbers below the surface of the shortbread and Royal Mile Whisky and he has refused to shy away from confronting it.

Rankin is aware of the ancient evils of his adopted city and, more importantly, the new crimes that fester in its arms today. But that higher state of awareness concerning his surroundings has always been there along with the author's natural leaning towards social issues and their effects on people's lives. Back in his youth, in Mr Gillespie's English class, when given the line 'Dark they were and golden-eyed', as a phrase to base a short story upon, Rankin chose: 'worried parents searching a busy squat for their drug-addict son.'[xxi] So there is the proof of that deep-rooted sensitivity to people's emotions that Rankin was born with, or at least understood, from a very early age.

Robert Louis Stevenson had the gift in a similar way and he showed it throughout his work, even his children's stories, both *Kidnapped* and *Treasure Island* being prime examples. We will return to Stevenson later but for now Edinburgh, the city Ian Rankin has analysed through his Rebus novels. 'I'm always trying to make sense of the place,' he tells me. 'And I try to do that through the books.'[xxii] But has he managed to conclude his analysis? Not yet. In a way Edinburgh is the heart of Scotland – it *is* the capital city – but it doesn't evoke the soul of Scotland, as Rankin is keen to point out: 'You've got all these monuments... and

---

xxi *Rebus's Scotland – A Personal Journey* (Orion, 2005).

xxii Author interview 14 January 2002.

visitors don't see the real living, breathing city. People say, in order to get the perfect city in Scotland, you need to take all the Glaswegians, who are very Celtic, outgoing and talkative, and put them in Edinburgh, which is a beautiful city.'[xxiii] So perhaps Rankin has to write more about other areas of Scotland and uncover their perception of Edinburgh in order to get a more rounded perception of his beloved city?

This question reminds me of a line from one of Conan Doyle's non-Sherlock Holmes titles, *The Exploits of Brigadier Gerard*: 'The folk glanced at each other, and whispered to their neighbours.' Surely this enforces the villagey type of mentality Rankin was alluding to earlier. In fact there is a very telling line in Rankin's *Strip Jack*, where he explains that Brian Holmes (Rebus's sidekick) lives in a village in Edinburgh, or a village absorbed by the ever-expanding Edinburgh. So in answer to the question: you need outside perception to make a clear and insightful prognosis of what's going on inside Edinburgh.

So you need the insider and the outsider to pierce the underbelly of Edinburgh? Yes, you need to talk to someone who actually lives there, and somebody who doesn't. And Rankin is both the outsider – from the Kingdom of Fife – and the insider – the man who has adopted Edinburgh as his home. And he can separate himself through Rebus, for he is the narrator, the man from Edinburgh, while Rebus is the outsider, the Fifer who took the normal career path of a lad from his hometown.

---

xxiii Author interview 14 January 2002.

And did this analysis start at the very beginning of the Rebus series? Indeed it did. In fact the first two novels are two of the most important in the series as they got the ball rolling. *Knots and Crosses* and *Hide and Seek* attempt to show the Jekyll and Hyde character of the city. But why is Edinburgh such a big influence on Rankin? He wasn't brought up there – he was taken there once or twice as a child, but his memories of the place really come from his university days and the awakening of his literary dream which, as we have discovered, happened simultaneously. And there lies the rub. With the growth of his literary powers grew his need to research and study his adopted city and one fell hand in glove with the other. Too tidy an explanation? Perhaps it is, but Edinburgh became the catalyst for his academic studies, and maybe that ongoing analysis of the city will continue throughout his work until his very last novel, because if it isn't present in the sub-text then the soul of Rankin's novel has dissolved. Edinburgh, its people, its 'villagey' aspects, are what keeps Rankin writing and interested in his ongoing crime series (note the plural); not just Rebus but any other central character he chooses to create.

Rankin's fascination encompasses the lives of locals who used to hide in the tunnels beneath the streets when the city was attacked in ancient times (*Hide and Seek* and *Mortal Causes* touch on subterranean Edinburgh), then there are the old boogie tales of Deacon Brodie, which harks back to the intrigue surrounding the writing of Stevenson's *Strange Case of Dr Jekyll and Mr Hyde*. Dark, true-life tales influence Rankin's writing, such as the little dolls in their tiny coffins found in a cave on Arthur's Seat in Edinburgh (*The Falls*). There he goes again, always driven towards the darkness – set in darkness – viewing the city from a dark hidden corner and passing comment, detached, fractured from the throng, an isolationist, sitting on Arthur's Seat during an electrical storm, viewing the city as it's exposed through every blast of lightning. Yet he is not cold and remote like an extreme Bowie creation, but attuned to peoples' emotions, aware of their needs and longings, aware of the motivations of the Jekyll and Hyde characters who walk the streets of the city to this very day. An over-the-top summary? Of course it is, but there is something Pied Piper-like in Rankin: people follow him, believe what he says about Edinburgh, its past and its literature, and this is the mark of a good writer. A great writer? Only time will tell.

It is said that you can take the man out of the city but you can't take the city out of the man. The only problem with that cliché is that it was written to explain the character of a person brought up in a city. Rankin wasn't, he was brought up in the Kingdom of Fife; but Edinburgh did sink its claws into him at an impressionable age, an age when his literary talents and his powers of analysis were growing and, strangely, when asked to describe Edinburgh, Rankin would choose 'villagey', so he clearly feels comfortable there. And there lies the beginning of Rebus and Rankin's fascination for Edinburgh. The city naturally followed his original hometown. 'Edinburgh is my spiritual home. I see myself in a line of the city's writers, in the tradition of Muriel Spark, Robert Louis

Stevenson and others...'[xxiv] It is Spark and Stevenson, more than Burns, Scott and Conan Doyle, that Rankin continues to refer to. He does it in his books and interviews and indeed his PhD was about Spark and his first two Rebus novels were – by his own admission – his own versions of Stevenson's *Strange Case of Dr Jekyll and Mr Hyde*.

Yes, Edinburgh provided Rankin with a clear break from his past as well as the catalyst for fulfilling his dream career.

Rankin has said that after he died he 'would like to be remembered as someone who tried to write truthfully about modern-day Scotland – and as someone who tried to be a good dad'.

I find it fascinating, but not surprising, that he would mention both things in the same breath, because along with his devoted wife, they are the things closest to his heart.

When I ask him what he loves about Scotland, he tells me, 'I love the people, the sense of humour, the attitude of mind, the landscape.' These are the wonderful things. Conversely, I asked him what he hated about his country and he replied, 'I hate that we carry a chip on our shoulder, a long memory of perceived past grievances. Never mind "Auld Lang Syne" – it's what's ahead of us that counts.'[xxv]

This comment makes Rankin a very modern-thinking man. Yes, he cares about Scottish literature and its place in history, but also its place in current society. What can we

---

xxiv From 'The Tracks of my Years' by Andrew Preston, *Night & Day*, Association Newspapers, October 24 2004.

xxv Author interview 26 July 2009.

learn from the Scottish writers of yesterday? How has Scottish writing changed over the centuries and, more importantly, what does modern Scottish literature say – what can we learn from it?

Rankin has been at the frontline of this exploration. It's almost become a movement, especially during the Edinburgh Book Festival. Indeed his analysis of Scottish literature has made him world famous, simply because it was needed and I dare anyone to challenge that. Stevenson was an incredible personality, his books classics in a vast collection of genres; and then there is Conan Doyle's character of Sherlock Holmes – in my opinion the greatest character in all literature.

Did Rankin want fame, though? In *Artworks Scotland:When Ian Rankin Met Jack Vettriano*, he answered this question. 'I didn't get into this [writing] to be famous... nobody teaches you how to deal with fame.' Some could cast a cynical eye on this but I truly believe him. On the odd occasion when I've praised him to his face (for *The Falls*, *Fleshmarket Close* and *The Naming of the Dead*), he has physically cringed and stated – as he did in *Artworks Scotland* – 'When people tell me I'm good I don't really believe them.' (However, I probably wasn't that forthcoming about the odd book I didn't like!)

Rankin is a modest man. A private man. A family man. And this harks back to his statement of wanting to be remembered as somebody who tried to be a good dad. I remember being present at his *Fleshmarket Close* book launch (Wednesday 22 September 2004) and, amidst the praise and pretence being showered upon him, he got very anxious when he thought a *Star Wars* box set he had bought his son had gone missing. He was prepared to go straight out and buy another one and, to me, that is the mark of the man: his family is more important to him than all the publicity and fame journalists and publishers will pour upon him. Praise is ephemeral; the love of a good family isn't.

Rankin has two sons, Jack and Kit. Kit is two years younger than Jack but is seriously disabled with Angelman Syndrome.[xxvi] Part of one of his chromosomes is missing. The consequence of this is that he'll never speak, he can't walk, he has seizures and is – despite being in his teens as I write – still in nappies.

Rankin's top priority is being there for his children. For Kit that also means organising a trust fund, so somebody can look after him if anything happens to Rankin or his wife Miranda.

Again, I have witnessed the sincerity of this love first hand. While having a few drinks with Rankin and other friends and acquaintances in The Oxford Bar one evening, I remember Rankin glancing at his watch and almost jumping out of his skin because he had promised the babysitter he would be home at a certain time, and then leaving at the allotted time. This isn't anything as bland as 'being under the thumb' – it's being serious about one's responsibilities, despite wealth and

---

xxvi Angelman Syndrome (AS) is a neuro-genetic disorder that occurs in 1 in 15,000 live births. AS is often misdiagnosed as Cerebral Palsy or Autism. Characteristics of AS include developmental delay, lack of speech, seizures, and walking and balance disorders. Individuals with Angelman Syndrome will require life-long care. www.angelman.org; www.angelmanuk.org; www.scotgen.orguk/documents/angelman.pdf

fame. Although this book is not a serious in-depth biography of Ian Rankin, I feel the above should be said (and he probably won't thank me for it!) because it clearly shows what is important in his life and where everything else fits in context below it, i.e. the books and Edinburgh.

> 'For my son Kit, with all my hopes, dreams and love'
>
> Dedication to *Set in Darkness*

Perhaps the writer in Rankin is his Mr Hyde and the family man is his Dr Jekyll! Ever disturbed a writer while they are writing? If not, be warned: Mr Hyde will have a word with you. It's an occupational hazard. Break a train of thought and aggravate the writer. American SF writer Robert A Heinlein once said several memorable things about writing: 1) that it was a good way to beat the system, 2) that it was a very lonely occupation and 3) never interrupt a writer while they're at work, as they'll bite your head off!

Why the last one? Because writing can be an easy escape. Like the young Rankin writing about the Fife he only dreamed of, it kept him optimistic and forward-looking and he needed to feel that. Stephen King has said that he has to tell himself stories and if he doesn't, he gets grumpy, because his stories are an escape from the reality – the real-life horror – of life. Not convinced? Well, let's continue with Stephen King for a moment. Once he wrote a story called *Pet Sematary*. He didn't want it released. Why? Because it was too close to real life: teaching children about death and having a young child die in the book, it frightened King in a very real and genuine way, especially as he had a young family of his own at the time. To bring the exploration back to Rankin: it took him until *The Black Book* – the sixth Rebus novel (if you include the anthology *A Good Hanging and other stories*) to include a real Edinburgh police station and Edinburgh pubs. To begin with, Rankin hid behind total fiction; it was a complete fantasy world.[xxvii] The unreality is always important in fiction because it is the fiction of a story; the contradiction to this is that's the very reason why this book exists – to find the *reality* of Rebus shrouded by the fiction.

Sometimes the reality of life can creep into a writer's work. A good example of this was James Herbert's *The Dark*, where a real-life court case focused him more on the novel he was writing. Herbert then used the anger he experienced at that time to drill deeper into the novel, making it one of his most dark and oppressive works. Ian Rankin has definitely written one book in anger – *Black and Blue* – and he has said that that state of mind made him 'really focused. My trips into the "office" were an escape from harsh reality.'[xxviii] Although his motives were incredibly different to that of James Herbert (for it was when he first learned about Kit's condition), the above does show that writers don't shy away from real life and hide behind their stories; indeed the stories act as a kind of therapy, a funnel, allowing them to cope with – work through – the heartache of their lives.

---

xxvii Strangely, when Rankin started a new series of books with *The Complaints* (Orion, 2009), he went back to using fictitious Edinburgh pubs out of loyalty to The Oxford Bar.

xxviii Author interview 26 July 2009.

So writers are impressionable. They are influenced by what is going on around them; their lives, the places where they live. Indeed, when Rankin lived in London for a short time, he set one of his Rebus novels there. But for the most part, Rankin has lived and worked in Edinburgh and that's a very important place to both him and his creation John Rebus.

> 'Then sore harass'd, and tir'd at last, with fortune's vain delusion, O
> I dropt my schemes, like idle dreams, and came to this conclusion, O
> The past was bad, the future hid; it's good or ill untied, O
> But the present hour was in my pow'r…'
>
> Robert Burns, *My Father Was a Farmer*

CHAPTER THREE

THE GERM OF AN IDEA

'Yet it was during this obscure period that the drama
was really performed....'

Robert Louis Stevenson, *The Story of a Lie*

Now in the light of this information, let us move into
Rankin's university days and the novels he was writing
at the time.

For approximately 15 years – up to the age of 30 –
Rankin kept a personal diary of his day-to-day activities
and, on 19 March 1985, while living in a bed-sit at 24
Arden Street in the Marchmont area of Edinburgh, he
recorded the fact that he had had the germ of an idea for a
third novel. He hadn't written any of it yet but it was an idea
that excited him. It was a crime novel.

Although he recorded the monumental moment on
19 March, the original ideas for the first Rebus book –
written on an A4 piece of lined paper in blue ink – are
clearly dated 15 March 1985. Also, towards the bottom of

that page, which clearly lays out the basic plot of *Knots and Crosses*, is the historic note: 'Hero – Rebus'.

And that is exactly where and when the character of John Rebus was born. Rankin was a post-graduate student at Edinburgh University. The lion's share of his time was spent on his thesis of Muriel Spark and teaching some undergraduate classes; writing was just his hobby and he had been moderately successful as an amateur. Along with his previous competition successes (he had been a runner-up in a short story competition organised by *The Scotsman* newspaper and won a short story competition run by Radio Forth, which was based upon a relation's naked afternoon stroll along the streets of Cardenden's neighbouring mining town, Lochgelly!) he was also busy reviewing books for a local radio station.

This was all commendable stuff but there was more substance bubbling underneath the surface. I mentioned at the top of this chapter that *Knots and Crosses* was Rankin's *third* novel; what about the first two?

To this day, Rankin's first attempt at a novel (and I'm not including the 40 page effort from his formative years) remains unissued. Apparently a spoof black comedy, which he jokingly told me he would have to dust off someday and make fit for publication,[xxix] the book is set in a Highland hotel and features a one-legged schizophrenic librarian, a young boy with special powers, and the abduction of a

---

xxix Interestingly in 2004 Rankin told me – and other reporters – that he would never consider re-issuing his first published novel *The Flood*, but did so later that year. He also went on to re-release his third published novel *Watchman*.

famous American novelist by the 'provisional wing' of the Scottish National Party. The book was called *Summer Rites* and still makes Rankin smile when talking about it today.

The book was rejected outright by publishers. One mentioned that the last third needed re-writing, something Rankin wasn't prepared to do at the time. If this was due to his confidence in the story or the pressures of his studies is unclear, but suffice to say Rankin isn't too sure where this first manuscript is now; there was only one copy and it was written in the days before he had a computer!

The impression he gives of this book is akin to a Tom Sharpe novel and perhaps as much as a departure from the style he has become famous for as his fourth novel *Westwind* (Barrie & Jenkins, 1990). *Westwind* was a British/American political thriller concerning a British astronaut called Mike Dreyfuss and the launching of a new communications satellite.[xxx] It wasn't until 1991 that *Hide and Seek*, the second Rebus novel, was published, some five years after the first novel and six years since the birth of the character. So of his first five published novels, only two featured John Rebus. His third published novel *Watchman* featured the journalist Jim Stevens, who had appeared in *Knots and Crosses*, so it was this character that had the first 'sequel', not Rebus!

It is doubtful if Rankin ever considered a series about a journalist but what all this does prove is that Rebus wasn't paramount in Rankin's mind for quite some time. Rankin

---

xxx All quite serious stuff at the time; if Rankin thought he was the next Frederick Forsyth is uncertain, however, it does go some way to show that he didn't concentrate solely on Rebus after his initial idea in 1985.

was keen to try other ideas and genres, starting with black comedy – *Summer Rites*.[xxxi]

In March 1985 Rankin was still studying the novels of Muriel Spark but in the Introduction to the Collector's Edition of *Knots and Crosses* (Orion, 2007) he admitted that his thesis 'was proving less important to me than my own writing'. He had achieved his first success. This explains the reason why the creation of what would be *Knots and Crosses* got mentioned in his diary on 19 March, days after being conceived. The 19th was the biggest day in his modest literary life: he had had a novel accepted for publication by a small Edinburgh publisher, Polygon, and had gone along to the publishers to sign the contract! The novel was called *The Flood* and it was set in a decaying mining village – his own childhood village of Cardenden – 'Carsden' in the book. Rankin and his teenage friends had once nicknamed Cardenden Cardeadend and local people became upset with Rankin's depiction of their community in his novel, which they considered to be as insulting as the teenage nickname.

The novel had started as a short story called *The Falling Time*[xxxii] but soon became longer, taking in a local childhood tale of a girl who fell into a canal against a backdrop of blue-collar Scotland. Still a world away from Rebus but based on

---

xxxi It must be appreciated that there is much humour in the Rebus series; it maybe black humour, but it is there. Also, any interview with Rankin is light-hearted and fun, so comedy could be something he could naturally gravitate too, even today.

xxxii See Introduction to *The Flood* (Orion, 2005).

the evidence of his earlier, albeit unreleased, work, *The Flood* made him a firm Scottish writer, using locations from his home country throughout.

When *The Flood* was re-issued by Orion in 2005, it benefited from a thorough re-proofing from Jon Wood (Rankin's editor at Orion), and allowed his legions of fans to read a book previously worth up to £1,000 in hardback on the collector's market. There were 400 copies of the original hardback printed simultaneously with 600 paperback copies. The book jacket – along with the editorial – was completed by students, making a modest first outing for Rankin but one that has endured and today ranks as one of his most interesting diversions from the Rebus series.[xxxiii] Some people, myself among them, consider *The Flood* to be a female-interest book. If it is because of the female lead character or the big emotions displayed throughout the story, is unclear, but that's the nature of *The Flood*: it is difficult to define. Rankin calls it 'a young man's book', meaning that only a young man could write it. He's right in the respect that it's a book based upon youthful memories – stories heard, locations from one's childhood town – and that makes it both different and endearing.

The Flood is not a crime novel. It sits on that broad shelf of General Fiction that is never defined and encapsulates those almost genreless tomes that beg for mainstream attention. It is an underrated work written before genre became important to the bestselling-writer-to-be, so it is

---

xxxiii In 2009, Rankin contributed a short story to an anthology (in support of the One City Trust) called *Crimespotting*, published by Polygon.

completely uncommercial in that respect. In fact, for story alone, it is a book I rate more highly than Rebus tomes such as *Wolfman* and *Strip Jack*, so it is definitely among his best efforts in regard to his early work.

On 22 March 1985, still buzzing from the success of placing *The Flood*, Rankin decided to start work on his first Rebus novel. He was living in a bedsit in Marchmont. He had a gas fire and an electric typewriter. Two days later he had given his story a working title: *Knots and Crosses*. He stared out of the window at a tenement opposite and decided that Rebus would live there.

The book opens with Rebus placing flowers on his father's grave on the fifth anniversary of his death (28 April – Rankin's own birthday!). He then battles through miserable weather to visit his brother who, although polite, really doesn't want to see him. Rebus's brother Michael has made a success of his life as a stage magician – like their father had been – and Rebus feels a million miles away from the bullshit and pretence of his brother's life. He returns to his job where he investigates a child-killer. Rebus starts receiving small knots and crosses in the post from the killer. It becomes clear that the killer is someone he knows and the story builds from there.

The impression Rankin wanted to give the reader at the time – now lost on any reader of the Rebus series – is that Rebus himself is a suspect in the story. He makes the character's life complicated; something he may have grown to regret as the series progressed.

Rebus wasn't behind the murder case but he did find out who was: someone who wanted revenge for a past misdemeanour. The killer had already killed the son of Rebus's superior, something he wouldn't be forgiven for, and now the killer is after Rebus's young daughter, Samantha.

Rankin had originally intended to kill off Rebus at the end of the book. It's an unthinkable thing to contemplate today; but all this goes to prove how disposable the character was to his creator in the beginning.

That said, Rankin found that Rebus leapt off the page while writing *Knots and Crosses* and the first draft of the book was reputedly completed in six weeks. Barrie & Jenkins took the novel after a second draft (completed in October 1985) and a slight cut was suggested by his new-found agent; something that was well advised, as I will discuss presently.

So Rankin's first Rebus novel was complete. Rankin had acquired a good agent and a reasonably large publisher. His career as an author was building well.

> '*Knots and Crosses* is a story of savagery and guile played out in one of the most genteel cities in the world. But it is more; an intellectual puzzle, a game, a captivating and accomplished thriller with a chilling climax.'
>
> Segment of the original jacket blurb to the first edition of *Knots and Crosses*

Most early novels are written during a person's free time, when the time available for research is minimal. For *Knots and Crosses* there were two potential roads for research, both of which were important in regard to the ongoing series. The first was police procedure. Rankin wrote to the Chief

Constable and was advised to talk to Leith police station. He spoke to two detectives who were apparently very wary of Rankin and his odd questions about child abduction cases – a real-life one being investigated at the time! 'In my duffel coat and Doc Marten boots, a Dr Who scarf wrapped around me, I probably wasn't their idea of a novelist,' he said in the Introduction to the Collector's Edition of *Knots and Crosses*. In fact this was an understatement, as Rankin was cross-examined by the policemen and the experience kept him away from police stations for at least the next year!

The second area of research was the SAS and, this is a very interesting part of the book to analyse, because this is the area where Rankin's agent suggested some cuts.

To begin with, Rankin credits Tony Geraghty's 'excellent book' *Who Dares Wins* (Fontana, 1983) for his research regarding the Special Air Service (SAS). As during his childhood, Rankin went to a book of a famous movie, although this time he was old enough to go and see it!

The first thing that strikes me about the cut 20-odd pages of *Knots and Crosses* (Rebus's time in the SAS) is that it's a watered down version of serious special ops training. There is a distinct lack of colourful language, a minimum of 'F' words and no 'C' words, just the odd 'bastard' and 'fuck', so the end result is both palatable and acceptable to the general reader.

In any area of the British Army (and its offshoots) there are always the amusing nicknames, such as 'Wiggy' for a bald man, 'Scotty' for a Scot' and so on. Not only is there a lack of this basic camaraderie in *Knot and Crosses*, there is also the distinct lack of 'creative' swear words, which make female

Company Clerks gasp and ORs snigger. So we are moving away from reality towards the palatable/unbelievable in this cut text? Yes, unfortunately we are.

I also suggest that Rankin used a little bit more than Geraghty's book in research, but the second-hand nature of the SAS sequence shows through. This harks back to the lack of time for quality research. With best intentions at heart, most young writers are not convinced that their early efforts at a novel are going to be published and, as a consequence, the resulting research is either half-hearted or, at best, compromised by the learning curve of the author coming to terms with his trade and the time available to undertake quality research.

Like the early work of James Herbert, Rankin's early Rebus novels are a little cut-and-thrust. They're direct, visual and slightly brutal (see *Wolfman* for a good example) but when Rankin had the opportunity to be over-the-top (with his SAS sequence), he failed to do so.

My personal grumblings concerning the reality of the sequence were probably not what concerned his agent at the time! More likely, the cut was proposed because it interfered with the novel's pace. The cut piece provides – for me – an unconvincing interlude that may have entertained the author at the time – and the die-hard Rebus fan in the 20th Anniversary edition – but did nothing for the original novel and the way the story has been enjoyed ever since.

Now I've completely slated the cut sequence, what does it tell us about Rebus?

A gripe I've always had with Rebus is the visual

representation of him. I've always found it hard to visualise him in the Police Force but strangely, not so difficult as a member of the SAS. He comes across as a hard-nosed Fifer −164lbs with no 'excess luggage' − a young man smart enough to understand when his mettle is being tested by his superiors/trainers, and somebody who would be cheeky enough to ask his 'boss' if he would carry his pack and jacket, as it was too heavy! This pushing of the system is perfect grounding for the police-inspector-to-be. His wry sense of humour, his been-there-seen-it-done-it attitude, gives him the perfect grounding for squaring up against gangster 'Big Ger' Cafferty in future novels.

Does all this imply that Rankin has let the visual image of Rebus slip over the years? No. Simply, he's refused to repeat himself and has let the character build and become more complex with each book through his cases, situations and general behaviour. Rankin has let Rebus speak and act for himself and as a consequence, avid readers of the series have drawn a very intricate and personal picture of the man over the years through his interactions − the ups and downs of his many relationships.

This approach has two consequences: 1) not everyone would be totally happy with *any* interpretation of Rebus on screen and 2) readers who take the books out of sequence find it difficult to draw their own visual interpretation of the character.

Rebus is not as clearly defined as Poirot or Sherlock Holmes, but the stories are as intricate and the locations are definitely more vivid. Like fellow Scot Iain Banks, Rankin shows a clear interest in plot and location and an almost disregard to characters in comparison. In the thriller genre Frederick Forsyth is guilty of a similar thing and both Banks and Forsyth have not fiercely denied such criticism in the past.[xxxiv] Indeed, Rankin says that he finds out new and interesting things about Edinburgh with each Rebus novel, so at the very least, the location is as important to him as the main characters – or one is defined by the other. And here lies a very interesting point: is a person defined by the area where they live? To a degree they have to be, but there are exceptions; such as Rankin and Cardenden, and Rebus and Cardenden. They are two very different adults (sic).

Returning to the cut sequence about Rebus in the SAS, I agree with the agent's call to cut it, albeit for different reasons. The cut sequence was a great exercise in Rankin getting to know Rebus, but little more.[xxxv] Or maybe one thing more: it vindicates Rankin's claim that Rebus jumped off the page while writing the novel, so much so that his self-indulgence was edited out of the final version.

The one thing I do take from the cut segment is the extension of the first-person voice. There's something very striking about Rebus narrating the story. An intriguing glimpse into his mind: 'He could have put me out of action in about ten seconds dead, literally. I wanted to be like him.'

This, where Rebus reflects on the trained killer that is his SAS boss, clearly shows a different side to the character we know by novel 17 – not a laid-back cynic but a man who

---

xxxiv Author interviews conducted 1999 and 2001 respectively.

xxxv It may explain why the reader didn't find out more about Rebus's character so early on; Rankin had already done it and kept it to himself!

was a born fighter and battled hard to get where he did in the Armed Forces and then the Police Force. OK, perhaps being a loose cannon compromised his career somewhat, but Rebus had his own moral code: he was true to himself. His principles were almost right for the Police Force and being a bit left of centre was acceptable in order to get the job done. And there is Inspector Rebus, a man at the outset nothing like his creator.

My parting thought regarding the self-narrative part of *Knots and Crosses*: now that Rankin has whetted our appetite for a first person story in the Rebus series, why doesn't he write a large tome in the first person? Rebus in retirement, maybe an autobiography (sic), surely that would expose more of the inner man, not unlike Jackie Leven's song *The Haunting of John Rebus*, perhaps with the same melancholy overtones. Isn't it time Rebus opened up and faced his demons? Surely alone in retirement the voyeur loses his protective clothing: the job that kept him so busy he didn't have to look at himself.

Knots and Crosses was a thrilling first outing for Rebus, stark, real and a good, entertaining read. Rankin admits that Rebus is a little too well-read in the story, thinking more 'like the student/novelist who created him' and listening to jazz rather than rock music. Yes, Rebus was a little stuffy to begin with, but every good copper has his pretences.

I find it hard to criticise *Knots and Crosses* in its first edition, because it doesn't try to be anything other than what it is: a good cop novel. It seems to achieve many things by default.

And what does Rankin think of it? When I talked to him about the book (on two or three occasions in interview), he always highlighted the fact that the reader missed the connection between the novel and Stevenson's Jekyll and Hyde – something he tried to rectify with the next novel in the series *Hide and Seek*.

Rankin probably had a higher opinion of the general reader than he should have given them credit for (especially in England). *Knots and Crosses* intentionally looks at the split personality of Edinburgh, from the tourist areas to the more scary backwaters that visitors rarely see. Rankin took the character of Deacon Brodie – one of Stevenson's influences when writing Jekyll and Hyde – cabinet maker by day, gentleman thief by night – but people didn't reach that far into the book to detect that particular strain of schizophrenia. Indeed it would be something he would have to make more obvious with the next Rebus novel and he did.

Rankin dedicated *Knots and Crosses* 'To Miranda without whom nothing is worth finishing'. Rankin married his student girlfriend in 1986 and they went off to live in London for four years where he worked at the National Folktale Centre. This became the interim period for him. The books weren't bestsellers at this time, Rankin writing in his diary that when *Watchman* was released the world was unmoved. It would take several more years and several more Rebus novels for him to give up the day job (approximately the eighth book, *Black and Blue*).

After London, the family moved to rural France for six years, living in an old farm house. But his adopted city called from afar and the Rankins moved back to Edinburgh,

CHAPTER FOUR

REBUS, IN THE BEGINNING

'Edinburgh slept on, as it had slept for hundreds of years.
There were ghosts in the cobbled alleys and on the
twisting stairways of the Old Town tenements, but they
were Enlightenment ghosts, articulate and deferential.'

Knots and Crosses

After *Knots and Crosses* was released (by The Bodley
Head), Rankin looked to Scottish novelist Allan Massie
for some reassurance. He did this because he believed that he
should have written an academic work not a piece of crime
fiction. Yes, he still felt guilty for writing commercial work.
Massie was quick to guide his charge: 'Who would want to
be a dry academic writer when they could be John Buchan?'
Again the sober words of the older, academic figure were
great reassurance to Rankin. Perhaps nowadays Rankin is
settling down to be the wise old figure of academia himself.
His TV shows lend themselves to the persona of the serious
thinking man rather than the laid-back crime novelist, and
his participation in magazine programmes such as BBC2's
Newsnight Review enforce this. That said, the man you can

meet occasionally in the Oxford Bar, in the backstreets of Edinburgh's New Town, is one of the most convivial of companions you'd chance to meet, so maybe he has a long way to go before the cobwebs start to cling!

Writing crime fiction did concern Rankin in the early days. Not unlike the horror genre, the crime genre has a pulp quality that is hard to shrug off. Even the two-billion-selling Agatha Christie is open to criticism. So prolific, Christie laid herself open to the criticism of 'formula' writing with her aristocratic whodunits. However, Rankin would happily concede that Christie didn't write his kind of crime fiction at all, stating clearly that there was no time for the reader to form a bond with her murder victims before they got killed off! A point well made, but Rankin has killed people off pretty quickly himself, completely absorbing himself in the criminal investigation itself – or rather Rebus doing so – as much as either Hercule Poirot or Miss Marple before him.

The key thing here is that Poirot and Marple were not police officers. They had their own individual – methodical – way of doing things but they rarely had people to answer to, and the constraints of police procedure that Rebus has to adhere to is an important factor in giving credibility to the Rebus series. That said, if Rankin found Rebus too bogged down in red tape he immediately made him ignore the rule book!

Rankin did make his job more difficult by making Rebus a complex character, but in a strange way that made him more endearing and a little less like his creator. Perhaps the complexity of the character has resulted in some continuity errors in certain books but even Dickens did that and as Rankin has had some of his earlier work – such as *The Flood* and *Watchman* – re-edited and re-issued them with special Introductions, he can probably now do the same with the whole of the Rebus series, tweaking them for posterity.[xxxvi]

What Rankin – and possibly his publisher – fails to fully appreciate at the moment, is the importance of the Rebus series to both crime fiction and Scottish literature. As a collection, it has been released during a major technological evolution within the Police Force – which is interesting from a cultural point of view – with the advance of computer systems, databases, the Internet, the introduction of the mobile phone and complex DNA testing. The early Rebus novels showcase the primitive Police Force of the mid-1980s, while the latter books highlight the technological advances made since then. The books will stand as a social comment written in real time during this exciting 20-year period. Does that imply that returning to the Rebus series in the future could be a mistake? Yes, or at least, water down the impact. He could quite happily make an appearance in any other Rankin novel but not as the central character.

Although this book is all about an author and his creation, it must be noted that it is the interest in police procedure and the underbelly of Edinburgh that has brought us to this point. Throughout the 1990s and into the Millennium, the general public both north and south of the border have been

---

xxxvi It is noted that the latest Rebus paperbacks have special introductions nowadays but haven't been meticulously re-edited for uniformity.

fascinated by emergency services series, both fact and fiction. The grim reality of life is good entertainment if it doesn't concern you personally and what is refreshing is the overall message that these TV shows convey: a positive attitude towards the hard work, dedication and professionalism of the emergency services. Frederick Forsyth has said that since *Dixon of Dock Green* the British people 'have empathised with the Police Force and that has endured through programmes such as *The Bill* and into crime-stopper programmes such as *Crimewatch*.'[xxxvii]

So how is all this relevant in regard to the early Rebus novels?

It shows that by default Rankin stumbled into the ever-developing TV crime/emergency services genre (the irony being Rebus hasn't truly made a successful transition from novel to TV!). Rankin had been putting tiny bits of himself – the areas he grew up in at least – into his books and was searching for the right direction, even before *The Flood*, but it wasn't happening for him. The audience wasn't there.

The fact that it would take him the best part of five years to write a sequel for John Rebus, vindicates this happy coincidence. There was still a way to go...

---

xxxvii Author interview 11 November 2000.

CHAPTER FIVE

HIDE AND SEEK

'Ye need a lang spoon tae sup wi' a Fifer.'

Hide and Seek

In August 2004, as a bestselling author, Rankin returned to his hometown of Cardenden. He was there to open a new road: Ian Rankin Court. Behind some of the houses he noticed a stream – the Den – where he had been taken on a field trip while at Denend Primary School. The memories of the overgrown wilderness made him reflect on how far he had come. Ian Rankin Court had been built where a builder's yard once stood in his youth. He thought of his parents who didn't own their own house; but these houses were commanding six-figure sums from the wealthy.

Rankin went back to number 17 Craigmead Terrace. The front garden had now gone. It had been replaced by a parking space but the street remained largely unchanged. He, however, had changed. Marriage, children and moving homes several times, had moulded the man the boy could only have dreamed of, including a successful career as a novelist and TV personality. Yes, time changes, to misquote Bob Dylan, it moves on like a gentle stream, babbling away across the years. Rankin also reflected on the fact that Auchterderran Junior High was no longer a school. It had disappeared just like his Sunday School church.

He toyed with his memories for a while, allowing the distance of his previous life to affect him, wash over him. Was this Ian Rankin's former home? More to the point, was it John Rebus's? The answer to both questions was yes, but Rebus had had a typical Cardenden upbringing, Rankin hadn't. Rankin had escaped, Rebus hadn't. So somehow the truth was much stranger than the fiction created.

After his 'personal journey' (the sub-title to *Rebus's Scotland*) it was time to go home to his new life and leave behind the mixed memories and influences of his formative years. Two years later he would be writing Rebus's retirement novel *Exit Music*. My God, what a life that character had! '…you can always console yourself with a couple more gins,' John Rebus would observe in *Exit Music* and, for him, it was probably the only escape from a melancholy existence. Not so for Ian Rankin. His life had been an extraordinary journey, due to his perseverance with his dream of writing.

I find it interesting that there was a five-year break between the first two Rebus novels, and that journalist Jim Stevens was the first character to get a sequel not Rebus. But the character ate away at Rankin enough to warrant a return, and a much better book it was too. Couple that with the fact that friends of his wanted to know more about John Rebus, and a little bit of luck – serendipity maybe – focused the way ahead. So in that respect Rebus became Rankin's lucky break, writing about the life of a working class Fifer to escape the life of a working class Fifer!

The first time we meet Rebus in *Hide and Seek*, he is at a girlfriend's dinner party feeling most uncomfortable. Rebus isn't one for making small talk. He has a serious outlook on life and doesn't suffer fools – or pretentious book dealers – gladly. He knows he should make more of an effort for the sake of his girlfriend – Rian – but he can't even manage that over the weekend. He has neglected to buy a new suit for the occasion and a book he bought for her – *Doctor Zhivago* – he has decided to keep for himself. He has also neglected to remember that she is on a diet and doesn't like lilies, which turns a gift of lilies and chocolates into a pretty bad move! He is forgiven, because after the guests have gone, he advances on Rian like a caveman and she somehow succumbs. Although things would get worse in time, it is good to see that the archetypical male chauvinist still got a result!

Like many older officers in the Police Force – especially in films – Rebus is considered a bit of a dinosaur. He lacks airs and graces and does things his own way, based upon what was once a tried and proved formula; he has just got too experienced.

Rian, and probably his former girlfriend Gill Templer, found Rebus's quiet strength sexy to begin with but under that hard veneer is a man who is perhaps a little too unsophisticated for them, and selfish. Although a little disorganised in his home life, Rebus seems to appeal to attractive women. Maybe Siobhan Clarke, his partner in crime-fighting, finds him attractive for an older man. It must be Rebus's manner which engages the women but, like his ex-wife's love for him, the novelty wears off!

In *Hide and Seek* we find that Rebus is slow at writing to his daughter Samantha, something which must have affected the girl as she has decided to write to him less often as a consequence. Rhona – his former wife – is a painful memory. He doesn't want her to find out that his recent relationship with Gill Templer has failed and that he had been promoted to Gill's level: Detective Inspector.

But is all of this anything to do with the real message of the novel?

The children's game Hide and Seek was the inspiration for Stevenson's Jekyll and Hyde. Rankin, like Stevenson, wanted to imply that the face hidden behind the hands of the childhood game was the sinister alter ego.

Rankin thought the comparison was obvious and perhaps it was to anyone doing their PhD in literature. Nobody, however, noticed or cared too much! 'Each book I publish is another small failure,' Rankin has recently said and with the public 'not getting' the connection between *Knots and Crosses, Hide and Seek* and *Strange Case of Dr Jekyll and Mr Hyde*, Rankin seems vindicated in this belief.

It's not that he didn't put enough clues in the text. There are quotes from Jekyll and Hyde throughout *Hide and Seek*; Rebus actually reads the book at one point. Heriot Row – Stevenson's childhood home – is referred to, a suicide note is a quote from Henry Jekyll's counterpart, character surnames from Stevenson's novella – Poole, Enfield, Carew, Edward *and* Hyde, Utterson (a lawyer no less!) – are used throughout. But there is more going on than that. As *Knots and Crosses* would doff its cap to Scottish literature past, so would *Hide and Seek*, taking on fellow Scot Conan Doyle's Holmes, Watson and even Stapleton (from *The Hound of the Baskervilles*).

In so many ways *Hide and Seek* was a re-write of *Knots and Crosses* but that was fine, because what Rankin was achieving with these two books was a breaking down of the tourist veneer of Edinburgh. He was exposing the crime, deprivation, hardship, blood, sweat and tears behind the tourist trap of the castle area and Princes Street. He wanted to show the Hyde of the city – not an individual person – behind the Jekyll and clearly it would take more than one novel to do that. In fact, it took the whole Rebus series to scratch the surface. It is – in retrospect – as though Rankin was attempting one perfect novel that would encapsulate Edinburgh and become his contribution to the great Edinburgh novels, in his eyes those being *Strange Case of Dr Jekyll and Mr Hyde*, *The Prime of Miss Jean Brodie*, *Heart of Midlothian* and *Confessions of a Justified Sinner*. What he failed to realise was that his contribution was a whole series of books that built in stature and each within it chipped away at the tough veneer that had grown up around Edinburgh throughout the 20th century: Hogmanay, the Edinburgh Festival – even G8 (but more about that later).

'Hyde's Club. Named after Robert Louis Stevenson's villain, Edward Hyde, the dark side of the human soul. Hyde himself was based on the city's Deacon Brodie, businessman by day, robber by night. Rebus could smell guilt and fear and rank expectation in this large room.'

Hide and Seek

Rankin's Rebus series was his Edinburgh-based version of Anthony Powell's *Dance to the Music of Time*. Characters jump in and out of Rebus's life through the string of books as easily as in Powell's. We even have a character, Rian, who Rankin tells us, was the same character who appeared in *The Flood*. So even the books outside the series help people Rankin's fictional world of John Rebus.

Apart from possibly friends and family, nobody would identify any of this in Rankin's work to begin with. Maybe this niggled him slightly at the time – especially the Jekyll and Hyde aspects, which he laboured on – but he had alienated many readers in higher education through Rebus in *Hide and Seek*: Rebus had a strong dislike of graduates who came into top jobs not knowing their arses from their elbows. The contradiction here is that Rebus didn't make it through the ranks himself, as he admitted to character Tony McCall!

McCall is a fellow inspector and kindred spirit: he has the ingredients for a failed marriage in the making to complement Rebus's already divorced status.

Even though Rebus is only in his mid-forties in *Hide and Seek*, he is almost isolated from his daughter Sammy (Samantha), at odds with his ex-wife Rhona, and bad in bed with his 'girlfriend' Rian. He is unfit, unkempt and frankly a bloody shambles, but still he manages to star in a further 15 novels, two anthologies of short stories and one novella (20 books in all). But still – in 2009 – Rankin will say, 'There's some unfinished business.' So the complex John Rebus still lives and breathes somehow: he hasn't killed himself off yet!

Rebus is the catalyst of Rankin's fame but more importantly he is the city guide who helps Rankin explore his fascination with Edinburgh and no other guide will do. In a way, Rebus is the Grim Reaper of the city: once he has exposed enough of it, the facade begins to crumble and the inner degradation is exposed in a much more comprehensive way than *Trainspotting* (because it has developed over a whole series).

I get the sense that Rankin is searching for the perfect Scottish novel to complete his canon, but he probably won't do it because he writes on too big a canvas. That is not a criticism, it's an observation based on the amount of books he has written trying to expose the *real* Edinburgh.

His fascination for the city and, ostensibly, for the Scottish people as a whole, has made him more inward-looking but perhaps that's OK because he is the only person doing it. He is the only person chipping away at the veneer, the only person doing it in an engaging, semi-academic way and assisting students as readily as writers and teachers once assisted him. He remembers where he comes from and this is ingrained into him.

If I overanalyse his first two Rebus novels for a moment, I would suggest that there is some guilt regarding the friends he left behind in Cardenden when he escaped to Edinburgh University, and that part of that guilt is featured in every

Rebus novel: ordinary people in ordinary lives who are unfairly treated. In a bizarre way, Rankin evokes the moral scruples of Charles Dickens: a young man made good who has the poor and destitute voices firmly in his head and heart. OK, maybe I'm pushing the analogy a little too far but I like to think that I'm at least half right on this point. There is an affiliation there, maybe not even that – an awareness, at least. When I asked him what he liked about Scotland, the first thing he told me was 'the people' and that is very telling. He is in every sense of the phrase a 'people person'.

> 'As a child, he had stolen from shops, always throwing away whatever he stole. Ach, all kids did it, didn't they? … Didn't they?'
>
> *Hide and Seek*

I do feel that the rough, working-class teenage years Rankin endured forged a socially aware novelist in his soul, a person we wouldn't perhaps accuse Rankin of being until at least *Let It Bleed* and the breakthrough novel *Black and Blue*. These two novels, along with *A Question of Blood* and *Fleshmarket Close* form the heart of his darker, angrier, inner voice. They are more politically and socially aware. To continue the Dickens analogy, they are his *Hard Times, Bleak House, Our Mutual Friend* and *A Tale of Two Cities*.

So in summary: *Knots and Crosses* and *Hide and Seek*, although they were never intended to be the start of an important series of Scottish literature, were the perfect foundation to build upon. In retrospect, Rankin would have made Rebus younger than 40 to begin with but, if he did, perhaps readers would not have loved the character as much, for the angry young man is not always as endearing as the complex, grumpy 40-something John Rebus became.

At the end of *Hide and Seek* Rebus is disillusioned. Corruption is rife throughout the powerful and influential in Edinburgh and ordinary people – good people – have been hurt deeply – permanently. So Rebus writes out his letter of resignation but tosses it towards the bin as Gill Templer knocks on his door. Does she want to get back with her ex-lover? He hopes so but as time will dictate, he will be disillusioned once again, the corrupt will continue to rule the city and he will continue to play his own small part in trying to thwart them. The sad fact is, by *Exit Music*, Rebus understands that he'll never beat the system or the city, realising that he was just another cog in the huge mechanism that is human life.

> 'To live in the world without becoming aware of the meaning of the world is like wandering about in a great library without touching books.'
>
> *The Secret Teachings of All Ages*

CHAPTER SIX
THE WOLFMAN

Rebus's story continued with *Wolfman*, a book that became an interesting breakthrough novel for Rankin, for he would write about London instead of Edinburgh. Why was that? Simply, *Wolfman* was written in London in 1990 and would take on influences from Rankin's current surroundings. He moved to a maisonette in Tottenham in 1986 with his wife, where they would stay until 1990, when they moved to France for six years.

Rankin needed a steady job and applied to become a hi-fi journalist. He knew nothing about hi-fi but he could write, so suddenly he was letting everyone know what hi-fi to buy! When he talks about the job now he makes it sound mundane, and perhaps it was, but it was still writing, and to practise a little journalism wasn't a bad thing.

IAN RANKIN AND INSPECTOR REBUS

According to Rankin's diary, he started *Wolfman* on 11 March. 'I've started, half-heartedly, a new Rebus novel... it's going to be called *Wolfman*, if it ever gets off the ground.'

His sense of apprehension comes from the fact that he knew he had a lot of research to do before getting the book off the ground. That said, the London setting allowed him to use common Scottish words and introduce them to a London audience, as Rebus would find England's capital city difficult to get to grips with. Conversely the unsympathetic London coppers have trouble with the accent, not to mention their own prejudices against 'the Jocks'. If Rankin endured this prejudice himself when in London is not clear; suffice to say he lacks sympathy with the city throughout the novel.

Wolfman is significant for other reasons, too. It's the first outing – albeit in cameo appearance only – of Morris Gerald Cafferty, the gangster who rules Edinburgh. 'Big Ger' would start making his name in the Rebus series from *The Black Book* onwards, to the extent that he took on Professor Moriarty significance – always there to tease Rebus (not always from the foreground) as he makes his investigations.

With *Wolfman* set in London, one could suggest that Rankin was writing outside his comfort zone, but he had lived there for a few years before starting to write the book and had left for France before final proofs and publication. More significantly, *Wolfman* was challenging for Rankin because the book was about a serial killer – the Wolfman of the title – and it therefore developed into Rankin's most graphically horrific title as a consequence. His editor at the time thought the book would benefit from a few cuts, so the horror aspect was played down, or rather left to the reader's imagination. Rankin complied and learned a very important lesson as a writer: letting the suggestion of horror play on the reader's mind.

Wolfman was a commercial novel because Rankin wrote it to try and break into the massmarket. On publication of the book he would proudly claim that he was now a 'professional author'. Couple that with the fact that he had recently won the Chandler-Fulbright Fellowship Prize in America, where he was sponsored to spend approximately six months, and things were looking good for the young man. Then, when life couldn't get any better, Rankin's wife Miranda announced that she was pregnant with their first child.

With his confidence building, Rankin pushed the character of Rebus in *Wolfman* a bit further, as he told me: 'I didn't know Rebus at all in book one – he was really only a means of leading the reader from one place to another. By the end of book two, I felt maybe he was going to be around for longer than I'd intended, so book three allowed me to flesh out his character. By this time, I'd also grown in confidence as a writer, so I stretched myself a little, and some of this went into the character.'[xxxviii]

We do get a few more nuggets of character description regarding Rebus in *Wolfman*. At one stage he is regarded as tall. His chin is a little saggy for a man in his early forties, but he does have a strong handshake. He doesn't have a very muscular chest. His gut and backside have taken the weight,

---

xxxviii Author interview 26 July 2009.

not his chest and arms. Also, he has a strong personality. In *Wolfman* he gives as good as he gets from the London Police Force and never lets his focus slip from the hunt for the serial killer.

> 'Her job had become merely that: a job. Maybe one day Rebus would feel the same way. But he hoped not.'
>
> *Wolfman*

The above line sums up all of Rebus's heartache. He always gets totally immersed in the seriousness of the cases he works on and, because of that, he loses every other aspect of his life: wife, child, less serious friendships, and becomes an alcohol-loving, junk-food-consuming, rock 'n' roll victim. Maybe that's going a bit too far, but was it all worth it, particularly when we note that Rebus has 'more ambition than ability'? Also Rebus has baggage from his brief army career; one can appreciate that drink kept many of those haunting demons at bay but he's still a workaholic.

> '... a quarter to five, everyone in the outer office had already quit for the day, but Rebus hardly registered the fact. His mind was elsewhere.'
>
> *Wolfman*

Rebus is an obsessive. He lets his job consume him. 'Rebus wanted to burst out: I read your letters, Sammy... so many cases to solve, so many people depending on me.' Rebus has a deep love of his daughter but he is pragmatic enough to know that he can't live his life doting on somebody he hardly sees, somebody – a teenage girl – who is forging her own life. His chance of a happy married life with children is gone. Squandered. Rankin has admitted that he is an obsessive – look at how many novels, short stories and other writings (let alone talks, TV shows) he has completed over the past 20 years. He is certainly prolific. But unlike Rebus, Rankin doesn't ignore his home life.

Where did Rankin get his original idea for *Wolfman*? While living in London, he had developed insomnia. One night he stayed up and read Thomas Harris's *Silence of the Lambs* in one sitting. He thought he could write a popular serial-killer novel in the same vein. The result was hard, oblique and slightly left-field for Rebus.

When we first meet John Rebus in the novel, he is having his rail ticket inspected for the third time since leaving Edinburgh. He doesn't appear to like the Englishman he is travelling with and, when he disembarks at King's Cross, he believes the air isn't as clear as Edinburgh. Also, on buying an A-Z of London, he muses that the population of England's capital city – ten million – outnumber the population of the whole of Scotland twice over. For Rebus, this wasn't going to be an assignment to relish!

Rebus is more disorganised and out of his depth than usual in *Wolfman*, but Chief Inspector Watson – aka the Farmer[xxxvix] – had sent him to London to help investigate the

---

xxxvix Superintendent Watson was nicknamed the Farmer because of his north of Scotland background and his, at times, agricultural methods (see 'The Dean Curse', *A Good Hanging and Other Stories*, Century, 1992).

Wolfman and he – Rebus – has to be on his best behaviour to do so.

More easily said than done for Rebus. We learn early on how he deals with people on training courses, when they're only trying to be nice. 'Take your hand off my fucking back,' Rebus snarls. 'And don't call me John.' A book of discontent follows!

Rebus arrives at the crime scene directly from the railway station, bags and all. He had overheard a conversation at King's Cross about a new murder committed by the Wolfman and thought it best to get to grips with the case as soon as possible. The English police investigating the crime scene are a little wary of him to begin with, but perhaps impressed by his dedication of coming directly to the crime scene from the station. But Rebus's thick accent and tweed suit mark him as an outsider and, frankly, that is the way he's always been, even in Edinburgh. *Wolfman* just emphasises this through his brief spell in London.

> 'He [*Rebus*] went through the SAS, that's the Army parachute regiment, did the training, cracked up under it, nervous breakdown, eventually pushed into joining the police, but was never really part of the police machinery – so it was nice to make him an outsider as well [in London]. He was pretty fit, pretty tough.'
>
> *Ian Rankin, interview with the author, 2001*

Living in London had provided another new experience for Rankin: jury service. The author found himself on a case at the Old Bailey, where he learned a great deal about jury procedure and the security system of the famous court house, which he wrote down. This horrified a security guard, who tore up Rankin's notes in front of him. Rankin thanked him, walked outside the building and wrote the whole lot down again while they were still fresh in his mind, and in full view of the now powerless security guard! (This was all good research material for *Wolfman*.)

Wolfman was significant for Rankin because it was a book about another city written while living in that city. It gave him the confidence to write under different – less familiar – circumstances and must have added to his skills as a writer. Although he wouldn't go on to write a book set in South West France (although southern France would influence an historic part of *The Hanging Garden*), *Wolfman* did set him on a prolific road of quality Rebus novels, which would see him turn from cult figure to international bestseller. Titles such as *The Black Book, Mortal Causes, Let It Bleed, Black and Blue* and *The Hanging Garden* were the much broader canvases that would evolve the series and make it internationally famous.

It was as if *Wolfman* allowed Rebus to grow as a character – and maybe the stories grow too, taking them away from the claustrophobic epicentre of Edinburgh where *Knots and Crosses* and *Hide and Seek* lived. Perhaps it's more than that: maybe *Wolfman* allowed Rankin to take chances – to speculate more in areas he knew less about than his adopted, much loved city of Edinburgh, and this spread through a much wider set of topics in the future, such as the oil industry in *Black and Blue*. When I spoke to Rankin about this, he said: 'I only wrote about London because I wanted to explore the city fictionally. Rebus seemed a good way to do that. Having done it, I didn't feel the need to take Rebus so far from his comfort zone again.'

Not only does Rankin explore London, he makes very perceptive comments about it too. The observation of 'the top deck of a midday bus' not being safe predicts 7/7 in a strange way; his comment regarding passengers on an underground train ignoring a beggar's request for help is nothing less than an 'astonishing performance' in a 'moral vacuum... that frightened Rebus...' Rankin claims that people in Edinburgh keep themselves to themselves, but in London they can be downright rude.[xl]

Despite the coldness expressed towards the Scots, Rankin had some fun with *Wolfman*. First he gave Rebus a little motto to keep him from losing his temper too often: FYTP, which stood for Fuck You Too Pal (also used in the following novel *Strip Jack*). Childish it may be but get this: it worked, so don't knock it!

More importantly, because this was a semi-gory serial killer novel, the final 'chase' scene is one of the most amusing and entertaining moments in any Rebus novel. It works almost as a sigh of relief against the horror of the storyline. The judge is a great supporting character too.

Rankin also had a bit of fun with his list of Acknowledgements at the back of the book. This was his idea of a joke, naming as many of his friends as possible, not

---

xl Rankin has since stated that the one thing he really disliked about London was commuting.

necessarily people who had helped with technical knowledge that directly benefited the story. For example, Professor J [Jon] Curt. Curt was a fellow postgraduate student with whom Rankin spent a 'boozy' year when he was finishing his MA. He was also part-time barman at the Oxford Bar and Rankin credits him for putting him in touch with the place – so much so that he rewarded him by turning him into Rebus's friend Dr Curt, the pathologist in the series.

When *Wolfman* was due for US release, Rankin's American publisher wanted to change the title. *Wolfman* was so obviously a horror title. Rankin explained that Wolfman was the name of the serial killer in the story but that didn't cut too much ice. However, when his American publisher suggested the title *Tooth and Nail*, Rankin saw the merits. 'The title seemed resonant, and chimed with my first two Rebus novels,' he would write in the special introduction to the book's 2007 re-issue.

A couple of months after the release of *Wolfman*, Rankin received a photo from friends in Tottenham showing the gloomy real-life subway where the first murder in the novel takes place. On the white tiled wall, somebody had written 'Wolfman' in six-foot letters. Rankin has kept the photograph, probably to remind him that when fiction provokes real-life imagery, strange people turn elements of that fiction into indelible fact.

'The Wolfman had taken a risk this time, however, striking in late evening instead of at the dead of night. Someone might have seen him. The need for a rapid escape might have led him to leave a clue. Please, God, let him have left a clue.'

Tooth and Nail

It seems that at the time of writing *Tooth and Nail* Rankin was content to make Rebus a series. He had enjoyed writing about the character, and people wanted to know what this maverick would get up to next.

Although there were parallels between character and creator, Rankin would state that Rebus was like the older brother he never had – although Rebus never gave him advice like an older brother would! When one learns that Rankin actually had a brother who died before he was born, one could immediately interpret the Fifer Rebus in elder brother mode, but Rankin remains unconvinced on this point.

CHAPTER SEVEN

STRIP JACK NAKED

'He knows nothing; and he thinks he knows everything.
That points clearly to a political career.'

George Bernard Shaw, *Major Barbara*

Rankin was enjoying himself and everything was going well, but with the Rebus series destined to continue, he believed that any non-Rebus novel should come out under a pseudonym, because his audience would be disappointed if Rebus didn't appear in it. This was no idle threat. Rankin did write three thrillers under the name Jack Harvey (his son's first name and his wife's maiden name) and those would be published by Headline. In fact, the pseudonym was so obscure in comparison to Rankin's mainstream work that when I called Hodder/Headline for details concerning sales figures for these 'Ian Rankin' books, the publisher swore blind that they had never worked with the author.[xli]

---

xli When I spoke to editors and publicity staff at Headline (and also Rankin and his agent) concerning the print run of the Jack Harvey books, I was told that a ballpark figure between 1,000 and 3,000 copies (probably nearer the latter) was printed for each Jack Harvey novel in hardback.

IAN RANKIN AND INSPECTOR REBUS

'The fan had been installed and turned on, and an
hour or so later Doctor Curt provided the shit to
toss at it.'

Strip Jack

Although Rankin has always considered his Rebus books to
be 'whodunits' or 'crime novels' he has always said that they
are also very funny books and that they made him laugh.
Although there are macabre incidents in the books, there is
always an opportunity for humour, if not in the narrator's
banter (see above quote) then within the story itself and
brought about by the characters themselves.

Part of the reality of the Police Force – or even the
Armed Forces – is that extreme circumstances need a
release valve. There will be natural banter between good
friends – and not so good friends! – and no one, with the
possible exception of superior officers, can be serious all
the time. Indeed, the irrepressible Dr Curt is a zany as the
manic Professor Professor from the children's cartoon *The
Secret Show*: he's always finding his own jokes funny while
others fail to see the humour, and he always delivers an
important fact.

'Rebus didn't mind being the butt. He knew the
way it was. In a murder inquiry, you worked as a
team. Lauderdale, as team manager, had the job of
boosting morale, keeping things lively. Rebus
wasn't part of the team, not exactly, so he was open
to the occasional low tackle with studs showing.'

Mortal Causes

A lot of the humour in the Rebus series comes at the good inspector's expense. His inability to have a proper date with a woman without things going pear-shaped (i.e. he is late, has been involved in a skirmish, decided to keep whatever peace offering he has bought to make up for the last disaster), adds a distinct injection of black humour to proceedings. Also, Rankin has a private joke with the real Police Force, because when it is time for Rebus to buckle down and do things in a methodical manner – i.e. follow police procedure to the letter – Rankin ignores the whole thing and says, 'Rebus wouldn't do it that way, he's a maverick.' Therefore he cuts out all the tedious procedure and red tape that would give stark, boring realism to the stories, and consequently have his own private chuckle with any reader who knows the slightest thing about police procedure.

The people who appreciated Rankin's dark humour from the off were his new publishers Orion. In the summer of 1992 they released a numbered, limited edition proof of his first Rebus novel for them – *Strip Jack*. High up on the back of the paperback they wrote: 'Memo to Chief Inspector Morse and Wexford. You have a new rival from north of the border. His name is Rebus, his manor Edinburgh. And he's found a writer as good as yours. Watch him.'

Tongue-in-cheek banter it may have been but it did send a message out to the reviewers who were keen to tar Rebus with the same brush as his rivals. Orion got the mind-set right for Rankin/Rebus early on and that probably explains why the relationship has been a strong one over the past two decades. Rankin echoes this: 'Orion was a brand new publishing house. The attitude was very gung-ho and there were lots of good new ideas being tossed around. To prise me away from Random Century they had doubled my advance (to 10k I think, but that may have been for two books). I'd already moved from Polygon to Bodley Head to Barrie & Jenkins to Century... If I didn't start selling, I knew I'd be on borrowed time! Of course, I'm still with Orion, so obviously we work well together – but that's the best outcome for a writer. There are people around me who've become friends and confidants.'[xlii]

Strip Jack wasn't to be Rankin's breakthrough novel, however. In fact, it is one of the rarest Rebus titles in first edition hardback. The book sold moderately well but mainly through trade paperback. It is a fact that sales concerned Rankin at the time, as he clarified to me: 'It was my first book for Orion, and I wanted to do well for my new employers! I was living in France and had become the family's only breadwinner. Our son Jack had come along, so I had to earn a living. I couldn't piss about. I was a worried man when I wrote *Strip Jack*.'

The title of the book came from the card game Strip Jack Naked (to keep within the game-playing theme of the first two book titles in the series), but Rankin decided that the title *Strip Jack* was more punchy. The title didn't come about because of the birth of his first son, Jack, although he became the subject of the dedication; his name had already been decided and the whole thing was a coincidence.

---

xlii Author interview 26 July 2009.

'"You're sure it was a hire car?" Watson asked
Holmes. Holmes thought again before nodding.'

Strip Jack

Of course the homage to Sherlock Holmes and Dr Watson
is there if you want it, and the irony is that Watson is the
boss and Holmes is the subordinate. Rankin is playing with
great Scottish literature again but he can't help it. The statue
of Sherlock Holmes stood for many years around the
corner from Princes Street (until they started putting the
tram lines down in 2009) and Rankin would acknowledge
Doyle every time Holmes and Watson – his Holmes and
Watson – took centre stage in his novels.

Strip Jack was released in October 1992. It is a political
novel about a local MP called Gregor Jack and it appears
somebody wants to Strip Jack Naked – set him up, bring
him down – which is why he is found in bed with a
prostitute during a police raid at the start of the book.
Rebus feels sorry for the man until Jack's wife is found
murdered and the novel takes a more sinister turn.

The constituency of North and South Esk (a fictional
setting in the novel) has parallels to North and South
Edinburgh but there is more to it than that. The book is
about boundaries, territorial/political, and personal ones
too. It hits out at both Conservative and Labour parties and
makes observations on the changing face of Scotland.

Strip Jack was the fourth Rebus novel – released after the
first anthology of short stories (*A Good Hanging and other
stories*, Century, 1992) – and it is clear that Rebus had fully
developed in Rankin's mind. He lived and breathed, made

his own decisions and pushed his creator on to greater heights. But it wasn't a dark novel, as Rankin admits in his Introduction to the anthology *Rebus: St Leonard's Years* (Orion, 2001): 'I think the ... novel is one of the lighter additions to the series.'

With a son, and the beautiful French countryside all around him, he must have felt more relaxed, despite the pressure of writing a quality book for his new publisher because, for me, that's the reason why the story is lighter, perhaps more laid-back.

The story is less dynamic than the previous three novels in the series. It is a straightforward whodunit but it doesn't go anywhere until Liz Jack is murdered halfway through. The only saving grace is dear Mrs Wilkie, the OAP owner of a remote guesthouse who is practically senile and provides a few laughs at Rebus's expense.

Perhaps the most important aspect of *Strip Jack* is Rebus's sudden love of rock music, which coincidentally is matched by Gregor Jack: The Rolling Stones, and specifically their album *Let It Bleed* (the album title will become a future Rebus book title). Suddenly Rebus's musical taste matched that of his vinyl-junkie creator.

CHAPTER EIGHT

THE PLOTS THICKEN

'When Great London Road police station had burnt
down, Rebus had been moved to St Leonard's, which
was Central District's divisional HQ.'

The Black Book

The Black Book was the first novel set at St Leonard's
police station and the first to feature Siobhan Clarke
(Rebus's soon-to-be sidekick). It also brought back Nell
Stapleton from *Hide & Seek* and the blind man Vanderhyde
from *Knots and Crosses* (note the 'hyde'). Also it's the first
outing for Sword and Shield, a hardline offshoot of the
Scottish National Party that returns in *Mortal Causes* (the
following novel) in a bigger way.

The Black Book was where Rankin really developed the
working world of John Rebus, as he told me: 'I know that
I'd been reading *Confessions of a Justified Sinner* in which a
young man gets too close to the Devil for comfort and
eventually is persuaded to kill. That's basically the plot of
The Black Book, isn't it?'

Well, not quite! The book opens with the black humour we now expect with a Rebus novel. Straight away Rebus loses a lover, finds a useless brother and witnesses 'the black comedy of life in a blood-soaked Edinburgh butcher's shop'.[xliii] All of this is dismissed by Rebus as 'just one of those weeks' but things get steadily more complicated and exciting. Enter 'Big Ger' Cafferty. 'I'd been reading Larry Block's Matt Scudder books,' Rankin told me. 'And Scudder becomes friends with a really nasty gangster.' So Rebus needed his contact with the underworld, his nemesis, his Professor Moriarty? 'Let's call "Big Ger" an "homage" to Block's novels.'[xliv]

Surely Cafferty is a little more complex than that? In one of my interviews with Rankin, for *Fleshmarket Close* (5 November 2004), he opened up a little more when I queried the big gangster coming down to London in his youth. 'Cafferty's an amalgam of several real-life Glasgow "gangsters". I've definitely read accounts of how such real-life '60s villains as Jimmy Boyle made the trip to London and did strong-arm work for the likes of the Krays and the Richardsons. This may have been mentioned in Boyle's own autobiography, or in one of the many true crime books written about the Glasgow underworld... I definitely came across the info somewhere. One of these days I'm going to write a short story – maybe a long story – about Cafferty's early years, written from his point of view.'

---

xliii Jacket blurb to first UK edition (Orion, 1993).

xliv Author interview 26 July 2009.

A young Cafferty book? Well, the path seems to have gone cold on that for the moment… but as for Glasgow-based gangsters assisting the Krays and Richardsons in the '60s, 'Scotch' Jack Dixon and Ian Barrie are very good examples of Scots who came down to London to join the Kray firm, so there could be an interesting story there for 'Big Ger' – or rather Rankin.

But I have one more observation regarding the London connection:

> 'A handy lesson with "Big Ger" after you. He really makes people disappear, doesn't he? Dumping them at sea like that. That's what he does, isn't it?'
>
> *The Black Book*

This scene is straight out of the *supposed* history books, where Freddie Foreman, king of the London underworld, supposedly disposed of the body of Jack 'The Hat' McVitie as a favour to the Kray Twins, by giving him a burial at sea. Giving 'Big Ger' the label of Scotland's answer to Foreman is credible in the light of his involvement in the Rebus series after *The Black Book*.

Rankin has mentioned the murder of McVitie a couple of times in his novels (*Tooth and Nail* and *Black and Blue*), and it is interesting that he uses Freddie Foreman's alleged techniques as a consequence.[xlv]

---

xlv If readers wish to know more regarding the East End perception of the killing of Jack McVitie and other murders perpetrated by the Kray Twins, may I refer them to *Getting Away With Murder*, Lenny Hamilton with Craig Cabell (John Blake, 2007).

One day, while drinking in the Oxford Bar, Rankin was told about a hotel in Princes Street that burned down in mysterious circumstances and, along with the memories he had of the smell of the breweries in the west of the city, he brought together the essence of the story that would feature a brewing family, the mystery of the burned-down hotel, 'Big Ger', St Leonard's and Siobhan Clarke.

This was the beginning of the grown-up Rebus. Rankin would consider that that happened from *Strip Jack*, but I think not. The natural break comes at the beginning of *The Black Book* when we meet Rebus at his new desk at St Leonard's. It is only there that the new beginning is complete, with important new characters and real-life Edinburgh pubs.

The Black Book is also significant to us in as much as it reintroduces Rebus's brother Michael. Michael is looking up his brother in Edinburgh after serving three years of a five-year prison sentence for drug dealing, as a consequence of the events in *Knot and Crosses* (the detail of the court case and the infrequent prison visits Rebus makes are not given in any of the books, which is a bit of a shame).

Throughout *The Black Book* there are tensions between the Rebus brothers. This isn't the self-assured Michael Rebus we meet at the beginning of the first novel. This man has been humbled and is at the point of rebuilding his life, relying, like so many other less-than-entitled brothers throughout history, on his sensible sibling (sic) to pull his life back together again. Michael becomes a pathetic figure and Rebus has more than one argument with him.

This development of character takes Rebus much further

away from Rankin's personal life, not because he doesn't have a brother, but because he has never had to treat someone – or be treated – in such a way, and there is no obvious connection with the reality of Rankin's life. This is another reason why *The Black Book* is the first 'grown-up' Rebus novel: the characters have taken on their own momentum. They really begin to speak for themselves – not just Rebus but Patience (Rebus's latest girlfriend), Holmes, 'The Farmer' Watson, Lauderdale, Dr Curt. The series is really one for the faithful fan by this stage.

Only if people were reading the books in order could they appreciate the way the characters interacted, the history they have shared with each other. In a more naive way, the same could be said for Ian Fleming's James Bond novels. If they are read in the order they were written then the reader makes certain connections and cross-references, which they wouldn't identify if they read the books out of sequence. Such is the consequence of reading series fiction: even through self-contained novels there has to be familiarity – synergy, continuity – between novels.

> 'The past was certainly important to Edinburgh. The city fed on its past like a serpent with its tail in its mouth. And Rebus's past seemed to be circling around again too.'
>
> *The Black Book*

The above quote echoes the legend of Edinburgh being built on the back of a serpent (also mentioned in *Mortal Causes*) but it also sums up the novel, in as much as it clearly shows that Edinburgh's past is haunting the modern-day city, just as Rebus's past is haunting him. It's like Rebus and his city are spiritually joined at the hip – as Rankin is with his adopted city? Maybe.

In a way, *The Black Book* attempts to wrap up much of the unfinished business of the series thus far and introduces a new real-life police station and real Edinburgh pubs too. This would naturally allow Rankin to explore and analyse *his* Edinburgh without watering things down through pure fiction, which is what he had done before. The reality has stood him in good stead ever since, especially regarding police procedure, as he told me: 'In the past I made most of it up. And the police officers started coming up to me and saying "I love your books but you got that little bit wrong."

'I started writing the books when I was still a student, and I didn't know how the police worked. I didn't even know that there were 15 people in a Scottish jury, I thought there were 12, like *Twelve Angry Men*. I didn't know that there were three possible verdicts in a Scottish court. You can have Not Proven as well as Not Guilty and Guilty. Not Proven means you think they did it but it hasn't been proved to the jury's satisfaction.

'So there was a learning process going on, but it became a lot easier when cops came up to me and said "I loved the books..." because I would say "What's your phone number?" and I would start pestering them for information, and it's got to the stage now where the police in Scotland are very friendly to me. They understand that Rebus is a maverick but they like the fact that this guy doesn't follow the rules all of the time, because in their ideal policing world they wouldn't have to do all the paperwork, form-filling – they would be able to get on with the job that Rebus is getting on with.'

So the novels are fantasies for the police force? Certainly quality fiction, as Rankin enthuses: 'The beauty of writing fiction about the police is you can leave out all the boring stuff. An inquiry will have lots of dead and loose ends. You get none of that in a book – you can hint at it but you don't have to put it all in. The problem with the cops who try and write books – and some do try with very good cause – is they don't know what to leave out. They put too much detail in and the whole thing gets bogged down for the reader. It's too realistic. The thriller is different. I used to write thrillers and people who read thrillers have different expectations. They want to believe that they're learning stuff and they are very techi-minded, so they do want to know how a Heckler Koch MP5 works. They want the nuts and bolts of it, every little detail. I gave it up because it was too much like hard work. Freddie Forsyth has got a lot to answer for!'

Despite all this, Rankin did have some fun with *The Black Book* (even though he admits that it is a darker novel than its predecessor). While in America spending the money of the Chandler-Fulbright Award, he visited New Orleans and entered a dive with an Elvis theme. It was here that Rankin conceived the idea of the Heartbreak Café in Edinburgh, an Elvis-themed restaurant with its 'Love Me Tenderloin', 'King Shrimp Creole' and my personal favourite 'Blue Suede Choux'.

It is irritating that critics underrate Rankin's sense of

humour. Despite the excellent – but dark – book jackets and the often grim subject matter, there is no doubt that Rankin's books possess a keen sense of humour and, to be frank, it is something prevalent across the CID when dealing with tough – and often nasty – work. The old adage of 'if you don't laugh you'll cry', is an everyday occurrence in such environments.

CHAPTER NINE

THE CITY BENEATH THE STREETS

'Dark, dark, dark. The sky quiet save for
the occasional drunken yell.'

Mortal Causes

There is a city beneath the streets in Edinburgh: a gothic subterranean cavern of intrigue and spine-chilling possibility. Rankin found such delights when visiting Mary King's Close in Edinburgh's Old Town (not too far away from Fleshmarket Close, which would provide its own inspiration for a future book). As legend would have it, during the 1600s plague was rife in Edinburgh and the people of Mary King's Close either died, or moved out and didn't move back again. Then there was a fire, so each end of the close was blocked and eventually it was built upon — until such time when the people of Edinburgh could make it a tourist attraction and inspire a local writer to write a novel about it! The book would be called *Mortal Causes*.

Rankin considers *Mortal Causes* to be a little outdated in as much as it looked at the IRA and its influence in Scotland. Maybe it was a tried and proven theme but the story was a good one and set to the backdrop of the Edinburgh Festival. Vanderhyde makes a cameo appearance and the concept of Sword and Shield is expanded.

Mortal Causes is a book full of religious tension between Catholics and Protestants. When an ordinary Edinburgh woman plucks up the courage to ask an Orangeman why they hate the Catholics, but rushes on before getting his response, we can appreciate how the people of Edinburgh hide their true feelings as easily as their macabre past at Mary King's Close.

Mortal Causes, like many Rankin novels, is subtle and showcases how the author can deal with big topics in a sensitive way. Maybe, with reference to Northern Ireland, Rankin had some help from his wife whose family is Irish, because he thoroughly understood the nuances of the different organisations that cause unrest and despair by their acts of violence and terror. Rankin observes and then explores this similar mentality in Scotland through *Mortal Causes*. He has told me that one of the things he hates about his country is how the past dictates a prejudice against others — mainly the English — and how that tarnishes the here and now.

There is a lighter side to *Mortal Causes*: the Edinburgh Festival in full flow, the Fringe happening on the street and being enjoyed by the young Siobhan Clarke — and perhaps endured by the older John Rebus, who seems to breathe a sigh of relief as the case ends at the same time as the Festival. The young and the old, history and the here and now, how the past influences the future: there are many avenues to explore in *Mortal Causes* and big questions to face. What is interesting is how Rankin does this without detriment to the story. He doesn't give the reader a Bono-like diatribe: he plants the seeds and lets you draw your own conclusion, while tying the story up nicely for you as his side of the bargain.

Rebus is totally absorbed in the case, as ever, almost 'obsessive' about it. Somebody has been murdered in Mary King's Close. No ordinary murder. The victim had been six-packed (shot in the elbows, knees and ankles), a form of punishment typical of the IRA, Rebus knows, as he remembers clearly his time in Ireland as part of the British Army. But unlike the IRA punishment, this six-pack was concluded with a bullet to the head.

Because he knows a little about the IRA, Rebus takes things as personally as usual – this is endearing to the reader but frustrating for the character.

> '"It's about time the tourists learned the truth,"
> Rebus said…'
>
> *Mortal Causes*

Although we observe that Rankin is 'obsessive', he is not as destructive as Rebus. He lets his books absorb him, looking into the hidden depths of Edinburgh for more complex storylines. Rankin doesn't possess the melancholy – the loneliness – of John Rebus but he does see the cynical truth behind the face of the Edinburgh Festival.

'He ... detested the Festival. It took away from them *their* Edinburgh and propped something else in its place, a facade of culture which they didn't need and couldn't understand.'

Mortal Causes

Nowadays Rankin is an important figure at the Edinburgh Book Festival. He undertakes talks, solo or with other writers (such as Neil Gaiman in 2009 and Reggie Nadelson in 2010), and he meets the fans at book signings. In that respect, he has attached himself to part of the veneer of the city but hell, you've got to have a bit of fun!

CHAPTER TEN

JUST A SHOT AWAY

'Curt got to his feet... "And now he's gone to
the other place."
"It's just a shot away," said Rebus.'

Let It Bleed

Rankin's next novel was *Let It Bleed*. He describes it as a
political novel. It is quite clear from the text that he
wanted to mention changes in local politics in Scotland as a
major theme, perhaps to take some of his ideas broached in
Strip Jack further.

The story opens with a car chase towards the Forth
Bridge in a blizzard. Rebus is more than a little concerned
with his CI's (Lauderdale's) speed and when an accident
occurs, it is his boss who is thrown through the windscreen.
Rebus is unhurt apart from a toothache, which develops
with the story!

What is life-changing for Rebus is his ex-girlfriend Gill
Templer getting temporary promotion to CI as a
consequence of the crash. This is a surprise to Rebus and his

colleague DI Alister Flower, as they think they are in line for promotion. Flower takes the news badly and conducts a swearing match with himself in the toilet as a consequence, while Rebus accepts that he is not promotion material and decides to congratulate Gill. She, it turns out, is less than gracious, mentioning that they have no emotional connection any more. Rebus accepts this to begin with, but it seems that Gill has more problems dealing with their past than he does, to the extent where Rebus loses his temper over her attitude towards him (and for once, not without some justification).

As it turns out, the men have more problems adapting to a female boss than the women. Siobhan Clarke seems to have a spring in her step with the sudden appearance of Gill Templer from Fife, but Rebus – who *should* be bothered – isn't, because the problems are on Gill's side, not his.

What is also significant in this story is, once more, Rebus's relationship with his daughter Samantha. Towards the beginning of the book there is a very telling phone call from Sammy. Afterwards, Rebus chastises himself for not being fatherly in his response to his daughter's general questions. If only 'life had a rewind button', he muses. Rewind for the phone call, or his whole career as a father, is unclear. Probably the latter, but Rebus wouldn't rate his whole influence on Sammy as poor.

There is a nice piece that concludes Part One of *Let It Bleed*. Rankin takes the most important characters in the story thus far and speculates on how well they sleep at night. It's a great summary of the characters, with Gill Templer 'unperturbed' and the missing girl '…' (i.e.

nobody knows). How was she sleeping? What type of sleep was it? Eternal? Rebus believes at one stage that she could have run away to London. It seems that 'running away' is a recurring theme in Rankin's books, present ever since his first half-hearted efforts as a boy.

'Edinburgh was a lucky fucking town.'

Let It Bleed

Let It Bleed is a revealing novel. When Rebus learns from Sammy that Patience's cat was killed by a neighbour's dog, he doesn't just lack sympathy, he carries on with the reason he called in the first place. This is more than just inconsiderate, it's Rebus being oblivious to the world that should matter most to him. Sammy had been blamed for locking the cat-flap and she is terribly upset because she didn't do it, but Rebus is wrapped up in the nuances of his line of inquiry and that sums up the whole reason why his relationships have failed him throughout his life.

There are two sides of the coin, of course. If Rebus wasn't so single-minded when it came to work, some cases wouldn't have been solved so quickly – especially relevant for kidnap cases where there is a clear race against time. So is Rebus unselfish?

Not by any stretch of the imagination! He's just totally dedicated – absorbed – by his work. And when that work is taken away? Ah, now that actually happens in *Let It Bleed*. The Farmer (Chief Superintendent Watson) tells Rebus to take 'a week, ten days' off. Not a formal suspension, but the next best thing. Almost straight away Rebus becomes melancholy, believing that 'police routine gave his daily life its only shape and substance.' Does this imply that Rebus couldn't – or wouldn't – care much about personal relationships if he had the time? Possibly, but then: 'He loathed his free time, dreaded Sundays off. He lived to work, and in a very real sense he worked to live, too...' Shouldn't this feeling send warning bells through him – what preparations had he made for retirement? Did he *really* want to improve relationships with the women in his life? And if he didn't, surely there was something there for his daughter?

Did Rebus care about her after the cat's death? Not really. More interestingly, in a later book, *The Hanging Garden*, we find, in a flashback sequence, that he simply fell asleep on a beach when he was meant to be looking after his baby daughter (but more about that later).

Do we learn more about Rebus's personality in *Let It Bleed*, with regard to making a connection with Ian Rankin's personality, that is?

Yes. Rankin was having fun with the character, cherry-picking little segments of his life and plopping them into the plot.

> 'But when Rebus's mother had been ill that last time, she'd begged his father for release.'
>
> *Let It Bleed*

We have already learnt of the death of Rankin's mother when he was at university and, in a flashback scene, we experience an equally painful scene for young Rebus, where he endures the dying wishes of his mother. Rebus's father is at odds with the whole thing, just as any other husband/father would be, but if we look at the reality for Rankin's father, it would be the second time he would lose his wife.

Although the scene in *Let It Bleed* is just a flashback, there is much emotion and one can't help but make the comparison between reality and fantasy. We know that Rankin will use the odd image from his own life to colour the characters and situations he creates. It's a natural thing for an author to do. But although Rankin can make Rebus endure such a thing from his own past, he turns things round and plays with him, distancing himself from Rebus, because the way Rebus breaks the news to his daughter that she had inadvertently smuggled bounty money out of a prison and given it to a bounty hunter (thus causing somebody's death) is less than tactful. In fact, it is stupid. But Rankin would have found that funny. It's part of the fun he has when writing a Rebus novel and part of the distancing he creates between him and Rebus.

Let It Bleed is a good read, its political undertones are plausible and the way the powerful and influential scare the echelons of St Leonard's is interesting, because they don't scare Rebus!

Rebus immerses himself deeper into the spider's web of political intrigue that is his case. He is accused – in different ways – of being selfish, but he gets so absorbed in a case we can forgive him this, especially when it exposes everybody else as a bunch of spineless bastards. He becomes blinkered and when the war is over, he looks at the corpses scattered around him and thinks, Did I have something to do with that? He's not totally guilty of being unfeeling, because he is not conscious of it.

There is one major criticism of *Let It Bleed*: all the threads are pulled together without the reader being given the opportunity to do that for themselves. There is something a little Sherlock Holmes-like, or maybe Poirot-like, in the way Rebus sounds off to the all-powerful at the end of the novel. You are made to feel that Rebus is being deliberately too speculative but it turns out he isn't. There are certain things he wouldn't know and to chance his hand as much as he does is a sure-fire liberty on the wrapping up of the story.

Ultimately, *Let It Bleed* showcases how perceptive Rebus is, but you do question that perception because you couldn't work it out yourself. Being in a big room full of suspects, there is something Agatha Christie / Conan Doyle-like in the revelatory summing up, which again echoes great novels past. But aside from this, *Let It Bleed* was a very good book and a worthy follow-up to *The Black Book* and *Mortal Causes*.

> 'Sammy gave him a good luck kiss as he left the flat.
> "We're not so very different," she told him.'
> *Let It Bleed*

Let It Bleed is a deeper book than its predecessors. The main characters are more complex, the supporting cast – especially tattooed thug Rico Briggs and smack-head rich kid Kirstie Kennedy – are both visual and engaging, but we find out a little more about Rebus too.

Returning to the theme of selfishness for a moment, there is an interesting point in the book where the Farmer tells Rebus – to his face – that he is selfish. He explains that he has had a bad weekend fielding scorn from certain dignitaries Rebus had been pestering in his investigations, especially when Rebus was meant to be taking a break (unofficial suspension). Perhaps Rebus feels bullied. He was, after all, only trying to do his job, but even Gill Templer thinks he had approached things the wrong way. She's worried for him, believing that he could lose his job by getting too involved with such important people, but that disappears with the outburst: 'I'm your immediate superior! I'm in the post barely a week, and already you've caused the most unholy ructions.' Templer still has feelings for Rebus, albeit suppressed, but she has now experienced how awkward he can be on a case for his superiors, and it is up to her to decide if she wants to continue putting up with a man who gets the job done well, but at certain – sometimes personal – costs.

Rebus is not an easy man to deal with, let alone like or love. He is a maverick, a loner, a lateral thinker who short-circuits the system and gets results. Because of all that he is frustrating and people have to pick up the pieces, but he gets results that others can't.

Moving away from the character of Rebus for a moment, there is a complex and political storyline in *Let It Bleed*, which builds and gives little away until the end of the novel.

Rankin is not an overtly political writer – well, certainly not in the early days – but when he did tackle the theme there was always a blue-tinge to his collar (working class not Conservative), which quite naturally stems from his formative years. He understands the human grief and suffering behind large chunks of Scottish industry closing down, such as the mines in Fife, Rosyth Dockyard, the list goes on. Indeed, this political sub-theme is expanded in Rankin's following novel *Black and Blue*: underhand dealings to rebuild Scotland's industry, as seen in *Let It Bleed*. Also, Rankin was a much more confident and competent writer at the time of writing *Let It Bleed*. Loyal readers knew what to expect from the Rebus series now and Rankin knew what he wanted to deliver.

So was Rankin suddenly writing to a formula? No, that would be too harsh. What he did do was weave in two or three storylines – different strands – and carry the reader through many twists and turns before arriving at his final conclusion. If Rebus's summing up was a little too far-fetched then this was simply because Rankin hadn't fully developed his new style.

Rebus's story continued with a grand tour of Scotland. It would be another book that would take its title from a Rolling Stones album, *Black and Blue*, and Rankin would crack that new way of writing so well that his ultimate goal of recognition for his literary efforts would finally be fulfilled.

CHAPTER ELEVEN

BLACK AND BLUE

Oil, a central theme in *Black and Blue*, is sometimes referred to as 'black gold'. Couple that with the phrase 'The Boys in Blue' (i.e. the Police Force) and you have the black and blue of the title.[xlvi] *Black and Blue* was Rankin's breakthrough novel: the one that made him an international bestseller, not just a recognised quality writer.

Shortly before the book was released, Rankin returned from his six years in France. He and his family were renting a house in Edinburgh but had to vacate it when the family who owned it wanted it back for Christmas. Initially this wasn't a problem as the Rankins spent Christmas in Belfast with Rankin's wife's family. They then spent New Year with

---

xlvi Rebus is also beaten black and blue in the novel!

friends in Cambridge. They moved around to other family and friends for a while, and while in York visiting friends Rankin read a teaser in *The Times*. It announced that the best crime novel of 1997 had already been written and its identity would be released the following week. Rankin's next novel was due for January release and he prayed that it was his book that the reviewer was raving about. It was, and by November, the eighth Rebus novel had picked up the Gold Dagger Award for the best crime novel published in 1997. *The Times* had got it right. Rankin had now truly made it.

But it was largely due to Rankin's experiences with writing 'scripts' before writing *Let It Bleed* that made *Black and Blue* – and Rankin – famous. There had definitely been a step up in the substance of the novels since *The Black Book*, and it wasn't just because of Rebus's move to St Leonard's and the introduction of 'Big Ger' Cafferty (although that didn't hurt the series at all). It was to do with writing technique.

Rankin had learned the art of script-writing and the fact that two or three sub-plots were important to a story. He had tried out the formula in *Let It Bleed* and refined it for *Black and Blue*, and this to me is the reason why the series then took off. Rankin doesn't quite see it that way: 'I think everything conspired to make *Black and Blue* a better book than my previous offerings. I got a strong central story and, thanks to James Ellroy's object lesson, brought real-world crimes and stories into my fictional world.'[xlvii]

In May 2005, Rankin admitted that *Black and Blue* had been 'written in anger'. His son Kit had been born in July

---

xlvii Author interview 26 July 2009.

1994, while he and Miranda were living in France. There had been no signs of problems with the baby either during pregnancy or the first couple of months of its life, but by nine months it became clear that there were serious problems with Kit. Frustrated by his lack of grasp of the French language and the punishment God had inflicted upon him, Rankin let fly his anger at Rebus and the new novel he was writing. *Black and Blue* became longer, more intricate and menacing as a consequence. 'The anger and all of that helped,' Rankin explained. 'I really felt focused… and Rebus becomes more of a believable human character – we begin to care about him.'[xlviii]

So the introduction of a disabled child spawned the bestseller Rankin had been dreaming of? No. *Black and Blue* was pure evolution: a sudden set of leaps up the ladder that had started with *The Black Book*, then *Mortal Cause* and followed by *Let It Bleed*. Of course the series had been evolving since day one, but Rebus's world had suddenly got bigger and more intricate, and characters were returning to the series, such as – with *Black and Blue* – Jim Stevens (the journalist) and Jack Morton (who had worked with him in *Knots and Crosses*).

We can also picture Rebus a little more clearly now. He is 'a couple of inches' taller than DS 'Dod' Bain, who is 5ft 11in, and he is also out of shape – if we believe Jack Morton, who has given up the bad things in life for a new fitness regime! So Rebus is clearer in his creator's mind suddenly, and does not have anything more in common with Rankin. Does this tell us anything in itself? Yes, perhaps. It tells us that

---

xlviii Author interview 26 July 2009.

Rankin didn't have to rely on his own personal background any more. The research he had done about the Police Force, Edinburgh and real life bad guys had made *Black and Blue* a real watershed novel for him. Rebus was suddenly the older man; Rankin had distanced himself somewhat and this distance had allowed the writer to bounce his character around a little more, take risks, become more creative.

Another very interesting and important part of *Black and Blue* is the character Rebus is tracking down, Johnny Bible. It appears that this serial killer is a copycat murderer based upon 1960s killer Bible John. The point here is that Bible John really existed and was never caught by the police. Rankin decided to work this urban-gothic story into *Black and Blue* (this is what Rankin was referring to with James Ellroy's object lesson), thus adding a speculative but very thought-provoking sub-plot that would engage anyone remotely interested in the Bible John case.

Using Bible John was inspired but surely Rankin was concerned about using a real-life serial killer after the fictitious Wolfman had had his name painted on an underpass wall? I asked Rankin if copycat murders troubled him (i.e. people basing their crimes on incidents in his book)? 'I've discussed this a bit with other crime writers,' he said. 'We feel that the people who read crime fiction tend to be very well-balanced – lovely people to meet! It's because reading is cathartic. All your fears and frustrations and any innate aggression are "earthed" by placing yourself in the shoes of these characters.'[xlix]

---

xlix Author interview 26 July 2009.

Black and Blue was more than a stream of consciousness emanating from urban folktales. It must be remembered that Rankin's social conscience was working hard nowadays, and the plight of Scottish industry/enterprise was something that stuck in his throat and hardened his stories. For me, this is where the anger comes in. Maybe the anger is also detected in some of the supporting 'bad boy' cast, as they are all a little more vicious than usual. There's Tony El, a man who likes to tie his victims up, put polythene bags over their heads and use power tools to torture them. Then there's Malky – aka Mr Stanley Knife – who fills emergency rooms all over Glasgow with his 'particular hobby'. Yes, *Black and Blue* is a more spiteful novel, and if we focus in on the statements about the decline of Scottish industry to the viciousness of certain characters and the cavalier things that happen to Rebus – including being beaten black and blue – we can see where Rankin threw his anger.

Sometimes it is only when a writer gets angry that he produces his best work. To adopt a cavalier approach to writing (or in the case of the great Goon Spike Milligan, a completely unorthodox/abstract approach) is occasionally the only way of breaking through the safety net. There are so many examples of this, from the ancient to the modern. It doesn't have to be anger that provokes the best work: sentiment and tenderness work too. I'm thinking of a book like Campbell Armstrong's *All That Really Matters*, where the author embarks upon a very personal story – not totally autobiographical – in order to touch his audience's hearts. Digging into emotions are the key to good writing and sometimes that is a very difficult thing to do, especially in crime fiction. Sir Arthur Conan Doyle found it almost impossible to do in his Sherlock Holmes fiction, trying to add flowery prose through his narrator Dr Watson, only to realise that Sherlock Holmes dictated a sterile atmosphere of pure facts!

> 'First there had been Bible John, terrorising Glasgow in the late 1960s… And now there was Johnny Bible. The media has been quick with the name.'
>
> *Black and Blue*

On reading *Black and Blue*, one is pulled into Rebus's life and interest in the Johnny Bible/Bible John cases, but that is almost the sub-plot to the book, as Rebus is forced into moments of happenstance[1] that pull him towards solving the case. It is an interesting way of writing a novel and the fact that it takes a long time to sort the Johnny Bible murders against Rebus' confusing life dictates and justifies the length of the novel. In fact, like *Let It Bleed*, things don't end up that well for Rebus, and this makes the story so much more believable – because as Frank Sinatra observed, that's life!

Rebus's flaws/hang-ups are clearly showcased in the novel too. The way he needs to fight a friend to release tension, the way he talks back to authority when *they* need to cross-examine *him*. There is a depth and believability about Rebus, as Rankin enthuses: 'Rebus is a man who has used his psychological problems to good advantage in his

---

1 Something Rebus doesn't believe in but Rankin does.

working life.'[li] And he is right. Rebus is a survivor. The fact that he had survived a tour in the Army, a breakdown, and neither drank nor smoked himself to death, is highly commendable. Could we say a similar thing about Ian Rankin? No, not really. Perhaps his drinking habits have got the better of him in the past but he is no Rebus, that is for sure.

Has Rebus therefore been Rankin's Dorian Gray? An interesting concept, but frankly one that doesn't hold too much water. Perhaps if Rankin was a single man, his life would have had less meaning and his books more, but even then I can't see where Rankin would have pressed self-destruct after the end of the Rebus novels.

> "'Thing is, I've tried to learn from you, but I'm not sure you were the right choice. A bit too intense maybe, eh? See, whatever it is you've got, John, I just don't have it." A longer pause. "And I'm not sure I even want it, to be honest."'
>
> *Black and Blue*

---

li Author interview 26 July 2009.

CHAPTER TWELVE

EDINBURGH, BENEATH THE VENEER

'But Edinburgh pays cruelly for her high seat in one of
the vilest climates under heaven. She is liable to be
beaten upon by all the winds that blow, to be drenched
by rain, to be buried in cold sea fogs out of the east,
and powdered with the snow as it comes flying
southward from the Highland hills.'

Robert Louis Stevenson, *Edinburgh – Picturesque Notes*

Although the Rebus books sometimes take place outside
Edinburgh, Rankin always brings the story back to the
capital city for the more dark – macabre – moments of
corruption and murder. A good example of this is the
novella *Death Is Not The End* (Orion, 1998). Rebus travels to
his hometown to help an old friend, Brian 'Barney' Mee,
find his missing son Damon. It looks like a straightforward
missing person's case (although Rebus is out of his
jurisdiction) but suddenly a Hibernian football player is
involved and the movers and shakers behind the
disappearance are the money men back in Edinburgh. So
Rebus is pulled back to his adopted city from his hometown

and, as Rebus's hometown is Rankin's hometown, one cannot fail to draw the comparison that Rankin is constantly pulled back to Edinburgh by skeletal fingers.

Too strong an analogy? Possibly, but what one must take into consideration is the fact that the passage of time sometimes doesn't heal wounds – it shrouds them. *Death Is Not The End* is a great little story for illustrating this point. Rankin asks the question right at the beginning of the story: 'Is loss redeemed by memory? Or does memory merely swell the sense of loss, becoming the enemy?' It's a big question for such a little book, but he takes the idea deeper: 'the language of loss is the language of memory… people leave our lives all the time: some we met briefly, others we'd known since birth.'

If we appreciate the title of the story in conjunction with the above quotes, we can see that death is not the end, because people have to live on after their loved ones have departed. Memory is both saint and sinner and keeps feelings fresh, for good and bad reasons. When Rebus accompanies DC Siobhan Clarke to a Hibernian game, his mind wanders back to his father taking him and his brother to local Cowdenbeath games to show that they could still carry on as a normal family despite the death of Rebus's mother. The teardrop of autobiography again in the story: that path where Rankin's and Rebus's worlds definitely cross over.

So memories, memories, memories: Rebus visits his old school friend and finds that he has married one of Rebus's old flames, a woman who appears more beautiful now than when she was younger and represents to him what could have been if they had got together. But Rebus – ever cynical – feels in his heart that it wouldn't have worked out. More memories, memories, memories but then present-day reality, for it is her son that Rebus is looking for: a lost person. And sometimes a lost person is never found and that is a fate worse than death for the people left behind. Do they mourn? Do they continue the search? Where does it end? Should it end?

> 'The street was dead. He reached up and hauled himself over the iron railings and walked a circuit of the cemetery for an hour or so, and felt strangely at peace.'
>
> *Death Is Not The End*

There is 'an echo in the bone', as Diana Gabaldon would call it. And one can sense that mixture of ghosts, souls – both living and dead – in Rankin's novella, all of them lost and yearning for salvation.

Rankin tries to tackle some big themes in *Death Is Not The End*. It was based upon a conversation he had with a friend, Otto Penzler, and the theme of vanishing, but as usual the idea grew into a more socially aware thriller – perhaps too big an idea for a novella, as missing persons is a sensitive area for many families all over the UK and can't be dealt with in 80 pages. There are many websites and helplines which try to help people locate loved ones who, on some occasions, just get up and leave for work and are never seen again. The National Policing Improvement Agency (NPIA) Missing Person Bureau (MPB) is one such organisation that 'works alongside the police and related organisations to improve the services provided to missing persons investigations and increase effectiveness'.[lii] So a very serious subject and perfect for Rankin's dark Edinburgh, but so underused in the novella and crying out for novel-length exploration.

The novella was important in highlighting one theme that fascinates Rankin: the people who pop in and out of one's life. The Rebus series has many characters who do this in the main character's life and in *Death Is Not The End*, while sitting in his car outside a cemetery, Rebus contemplates this. He thinks about his parents and stories about the neighbouring village of Bowhill: mining tragedies, a girl found dead in a river (see *The Flood*), a 20-something football star whose life was too short. There is melancholy throughout the Rebus series, as if all the characters are hiding their inner sadness, their own personal struggle in life, from the world around them. Rankin says that people in Edinburgh keep themselves to themselves and that is something that really comes through in the books. Rebus certainly doesn't like people getting too close to him, not physically but mentally. People have done so in the past. His old school pal's wife was close to Rebus and when she asks him to go to a dance with her and her husband – which he declines – there is more being suggested by the author than meets the eye.

When Rebus leaves them and starts to contemplate his life, we can detect a strong analogy between the Rebus

ii www.npia.police.uk

series and Anthony Powell's *Dance to the Music of Time* series. 'The structure of that book is interesting,' Rankin explained. 'Five years and five books apart you can have a character come in you vaguely remember... and these people keep coming back into your life. Powell said it's very much like a dance, and that's what the Rebus books are like and that's what life is like.'[liii]

Is that important for a series such as Rebus?

'I think so,' Rankin says. 'I find characters that I used books ago that will be useful to me again. It's important to keep a whole life [Rebus's] in my head.'[liv]

In the Afterword to *Death Is Not The End* Rankin admits that he 'cannibalised' part of the story for a sub-plot in his next novel *Dead Souls* (Orion, 1999). Some would argue that he did slightly more than this, but it doesn't matter – Rankin had an obligation to a larger story and the fulfilment of that obligation made one of his most popular Rebus novels.

Dead Souls would include some of the same characters and theme as *Death Is Not The End*, with Brian Mee getting back in touch with Rebus to find his missing son, but then things get much more complex. A paedophile and a vigilante appear, and putting them against the backdrop of Edinburgh bodes for a very dark outing for Rebus. The opening of the novel is a strong and dark one: there is a menacing visual image of Edinburgh Castle atop its 'volcanic plug', followed by a dark scene at Arthur's Seat with a man – Rebus? –

---

liii Author interview 14 January 2002.

liv Author interview 14 January 2002.

contemplating a headless coach-driver waiting for him, but left with the prospect that he'll never see his daughter again. Deep metaphors indeed. Edinburgh's Hyde clearly depicted in a page and a half, the perfect opener for a macabre story. 'I'm always attracted to the dark side,' Rankin says.[lv] 'Living as I had done in a succession of dreary flats, motels and high-rise blocks, yet researching my PhD each day in the grand surroundings of the National Library and Central Library, Edinburgh really did seem a divided city to me.'[lvi]

Rankin harks back to his university days and shows clearly that the use of gothic imagery is important to describing the underbelly of Edinburgh, like Stevenson's Jekyll and Hyde and like the work of James Hogg. At the beginning of *Dead Souls* (along with Stevenson's *The Body Snatchers*), Hogg's *The Private Memoirs and Confessions of a Justified Sinner* (1824) claims an important influence. It's as though Rankin finds it hard to write without the heady influence of Edinburgh's former writers, something he sort of confessed in an *Evening News* interview: 'I owe a great debt to Robert Louis Stevenson and to the city of his birth. In a way they both changed my life. Without Edinburgh's split nature, Stevenson might never have dreamt up Jekyll and Hyde.' And without Jekyll and Hyde, Rankin might not have come up with his 'alter ego detective' as he so readily admits when discussing both *Knots and Crosses* and *Hide and Seek*. But what does all of this tell us? Rankin needs the large

---

lv Author interview 14 January 2002.

lvi *The Evening News.*

canvas of a novel to fully explore an idea. A novella or a short story isn't big enough. Edinburgh itself has to be a backdrop to Rebus's work: Kirkcaldy, Glasgow, indeed anywhere else, is a respite from the true exploration that Rankin is going through with the books. And what is that? Answer: adding to the catalogue of Scottish writers and Scottish writing, making sense of Scotland's capital city and sharing his memories while analysing the multi-faceted character of his long-running detective – John Rebus.

Dead Souls, like *Mortal Causes*, digs deep into what lies beneath Edinburgh's veneer. It also shows clearly that the novella and short story don't give Rankin the opportunity – in theme or word count – to analyse the big questions he asks himself before putting finger to keyboard. *Dead Souls* was the novel *Death Is Not The End* should have been, but Edinburgh was missing and the lost lad had to call home.

Unfortunately, Rebus's problems with personal relationships continue, so he finds solace in his paperwork and the promise of a cup of tea. Well, that's the gist of *Death Is Not The End* – what about *Dead Souls*? The ghost of Jack Morton is in Rebus's dreams and a part-time poisoner is terrorising the local zoo where Rebus finds Darren Rough, a known paedophile. Then there's Cary Oakes, a US serial killer who decides to settle down in Edinburgh. Rebus's old foe, journalist Jim Stevens, gets drawn into Oakes' world and is suitably embarrassed, and then there's the sub-plot of Janice and Brian and their teenage missing son and Janice's need for the Ghost of Rebus Past.

The larger canvas of *Dead Souls* is far more satisfying than the preceding novella, and the various threads are worked through methodically to their natural conclusions, which are more melancholy than satisfying. Souls are laid to rest while living people remain haunted by what has happened to them, both through the course of the book and, before then, in their own pasts.

My only observation about Rankin writing a novel based upon one of his novellas is that perhaps by doing so (i.e. having a sub-plot already clear in his mind) he had too much time to write the novel and put far too many players into it along with other main and sub-themes.

Dead Souls isn't a book you can drop in and out of. There's too much going on in it. Is this a criticism? Possibly. Indeed when I speak to Rankin about his favourite books in the series, it's mainly *Knots and Crosses, Hide and Seek, Let It Bleed* and *Black and Blue* that get top billings. That said, there's a lot of reference in *Rebus's Scotland* to *Dead Souls*, which suggests it's a pivotal work in Rankin's understanding of Edinburgh and Rebus. Edinburgh is a city with a lot of hustle and bustle and with *Dead Souls*, Rankin created a story that reflected the brutality of the city, that would expose the corruption that lies beneath and go a long way to achieving the ultimate goal of the series. *Black and Blue* picked up many plaudits, but *Dead Souls* took the series further by getting to grips with one of the major themes: Edinburgh (*Black and Blue* was an out-of-town novel and couldn't do that). Also, with regard to *Black and Blue*, Siobhan was almost an afterthought, which is something quite unusual for the series; Rankin really picked on Rebus in that novel and simply left Siobhan alone.

So finally we understand that *Dead Souls* is more of an

important novel to the Rebus series than one initially thinks. It has less power as a stand-alone novel: it's more of the corporate glue of the series. Rankin almost acknowledges this by failing to list it amongst his favourites but quoting from it heavily in *Rebus's Scotland*.

All series need a book that pulls themes together. J K Rowling had to do it in Harry Potter (*The Half-Blood Prince*) and Anthony Powell did it constantly in *Dance to the Music of Time*. Also, Rebus is a reflective character: perhaps it goes with the job, but memories make the man. It's not a new theme or idea. Charles Dickens wrote a whole Christmas novella about the concept of a man – a chemist called Redlaw – having his pain/melancholy taken away from him. In Dickens' *The Haunted Man and the Ghost's Bargain* (Chapman and Hall, 1848) Redlaw turns into a bitter, hard, cold man as a consequence. Redemption happens when Redlaw's memories are restored and the moral of the story comes through: Redlaw was a better man for carrying his pain – his humility. Perhaps the same can be said for Rebus.

> 'Rebus hadn't thought of himself as the kind to spend long nights with the family album, using it as a crutch to memory, always with the fear that remembrance would yield to sentiment.'
>
> *Death Is Not The End*

CHAPTER THIRTEEN
A SHORT INTERLUDE

'"To the curious incident of the dog in the night-time."
"The dog did nothing in the night-time."
"That was the curious incident," remarked
Sherlock Holmes.'

Sir Arthur Conan Doyle, 'The Adventure of Silver Blaze' from
The Memoirs of Sherlock Holmes

So Rankin can only use Rebus in the medium of a novel? For the ongoing exploration of Edinburgh, yes, because only by using the larger canvas can Rankin tackle Rebus, Edinburgh and the multi-layered story. Of course, there have been some good short Rebus stories but they add little to the overall life-story of Rebus — well, apart from the odd snippet: 'He [Rebus] could not escape the fact that he had been born a Protestant; but his mother, a religious woman, had died young, and his father had been indifferent.'

The above segment from 'Seeing Things' (*A Good Hanging and other stories* — the first Rebus anthology of short stories) could echo Rankin's own life but it's just an echo, a minute piece of story that isn't taken further because the medium of the short story doesn't allow it.

Turning to *A Good Hanging and other stories*, the one thing I do detect in stories such as 'Playback', 'The Dean Curse' and 'The Gentlemen's Club' (to name but three) is Rebus's anger, which is normally pointed towards the more privileged classes – well, that's where we see it at its fiercest. Conversely, when others take the words of a down-and-out with a pinch of salt ('Being Frank'), Rebus remembers something the character says and stops a burglary in his very own block of flats! So the anthology of Rebus stories perhaps allows us to appreciate Rebus's little quirks more fully by their repetition – consistency – of feelings over a dozen or so short stories.

There are a few returning characters in the short stories, such as London-based counterpart George Flight (*Tooth and Nail*) who becomes a useful contact. But what I find interesting in the story 'A Good Hanging' is Brian Holmes' assessment of himself in comparison to Rebus. He considers himself two steps behind the great detective (almost a Watson, not a Holmes), but then remembers that there was a character better than him at school and he finally overtook him. Was this Rankin's way of telling the audience that Brian was moving on? Maybe not, but perhaps short fiction allowed Rankin to study some of the minutiae of the ever-broadening series, the lives of some of the secondary characters and what was happening to them.

Moving away from the content of the stories, Rankin admits that he rarely has time to write short fiction nowadays. Sometimes after completing a novel he will write one or two but it's not something he dedicates much time to. This is probably because there isn't the same market for anthologies of short stories as there is for novels. It's a fact that astonishes him, as he thought city-dwellers at least would find short stories more user friendly because they can be easily read while travelling on a bus or tube, but in reality it doesn't work out that way. Commuters – the general readers – wish to know what the grand theme of a novel is and take their time going through it. It is a more preferable pastime than taking 12 to 15 smaller undisclosed themes in an anthology of short stories. In short, the reader wants something they can get their teeth into and lose themselves in the unreality of the ongoing story.

This probably explains why there have been only two anthologies of Rebus stories, *A Good Hanging and other stories* and *Beggars Banquet* (that's not including *The Complete Short Stories* with its bonus story).

So can we say that Ian Rankin, a prize-winning short story writer, hasn't really shown his true potential in the sub-genre of short stories? Of course not. There have been some excellent Rebus short stories, 'Sunday', 'Herbert in Motion' and the fun 'No Sanity Clause' to name but three, but there does seem to be something ephemeral about the whole idea of the short story nowadays that makes it a lesser work. Gone are the days of Conan Doyle and the next riveting issue of *The Strand Magazine*, featuring the next exciting adventure of Sherlock Holmes.

At the turn of the 20th century the public didn't really know if a short story or a novel featuring one of their favourite characters would be serialised next, but because they were buying a periodical it didn't really matter. They enjoyed being surprised. Nowadays, with life at a faster pace, the ordinary punter wants to read the jacket blurb of a book and understand what they are spending their time and money on – they either sign up to it or they don't. The same can be said for television and a good example of that is the science fiction show *Dr Who*. In the 1960s when William Hartnell and Patrick Troughton took the main role, the average story length was six episodes. That was six consecutive weeks of 25-minute episodes. Nowadays the Doctor has to sort the universe out in one 50-minute episode. Only occasionally – when a gripping foe can capture the audience – will a story span two episodes. People will sign up to the ready-made meal and spend their money accordingly. It's all about packaging, understanding what the consumer wants. They'll sit there for 50 minutes and watch TV, but rarely will they want to follow the same story in bite-sized chunks over several weeks. Likewise, they don't want many different stories in one book with no overall pay-off: they need something to get their teeth into.

Perhaps Rankin should write a lengthy anthology of short stories, build them up over the next six or seven years and release a heady tome. Maybe that way, without the constraints of Rebus being in them all, will he win the short story battle. If the anthology has an overall theme, say Edinburgh, exploring a multitude of different lifestyles and events, will he come somewhere close to a diverse novel-type of theme. It could be a very interesting – and perhaps humorous way – of seeing Rebus in retirement (through one or two stories).

Am I implying by all of this that Rebus has stifled Rankin's creativity? That he has taken Rankin away from more

CHAPTER FOURTEEN

YOU GOT THE SILVER

'There is nothing I think very exceptional in my situation
as a mental worker. Entanglement is our common lot.'

Experiment in Autobiography, Being the Autobiography of H G Wells

The Hanging Garden is one of the most underrated novels
in the Rebus series. We first encounter our hero saying
goodbye to his daughter after a pizza. His obvious affection
for her in juxtaposition to the manacles of his job is clear:
they have cancelled their dinner appointment many times
because of his calls to duty, but she understands and he is
grateful for that. Rebus knows he doesn't see her enough
but he's pleased that she has a level of self-confidence –
independence – and is building her life normally with a
boyfriend and no apparent mental scars after the break-up
of the parental home. There is a sense of relief and
gratitude in Rebus's attitude before he gets entangled
straight away with a surveillance-gone-wrong and a
gangland hospital case!

Rebus is the archetypical professional copper, overworked and underpaid, who lives in a flat he detests and not just because of the student parties next door. He is forever searching for fulfilment in life: love, home, lifestyle and job, but is destined – or determined – never to achieve it. Although clichéd, this situation is typical of a large proportion of working people, not just civil servants and people in the emergency services. The unfulfilment of life is there throughout society and exposing that, discussing that and seeing people try to wriggle out of that is one of the main strengths of the Rebus series. Rankin's audience can identify with that. It is this accessibility that is key to the commercial success of the series.

Rebus gets under the skin of life. He looks under the stone and examines what wriggles beneath. Then he gives it a prod to irritate it and this is where readers delight in the character's exploits. When Rebus is confronted with a lawyer representing a gangland victim in *The Hanging Garden*, he quickly sees through the facade, understanding straight away that he is only there to ensure the victim doesn't give any secrets away. 'We're here to listen to whatever bunch of shite the two of you eventually concoct for our delectation...' Rebus says. This hard-nosed approach to his work is unconventional but effective, but it has made Rebus as many enemies as friends during his working life. Interestingly, *The Hanging Garden* introduces us to another side of Rebus's personality, when he suddenly finds himself looking at his daughter unconscious on a bed, the victim of a hit-and-run.

The shock, anger and despair of a loving parent are suddenly brought to the fore. Rebus forgets momentarily that he is a policeman. He is now a victim's father and he pounds a wall and demands immediate justice. When he calms down he realises that Rhona – his ex-wife – is exclusively responsible for his daughter's good upbringing. A memory of his fatherly responsibilities on a family holiday vindicates this: he was left in charge of his baby daughter as she buried his feet in the sand. He fell asleep and woke up with her missing. Rhona was distraught. They found Sammy in a hollow in a sand dune. They pulled her out. Rebus punched the roof of the dune and the whole thing collapsed; his daughter could have been killed or buried alive and it would have been his fault. But was it his fault now? Was the accident a deliberate stab at Rebus from someone with a grudge?

If ever the Jekyll and Hyde side to Rebus's personality was exposed in a novel, this is it. There is the normal everyday love for his daughter and dedication to his work; then there is the ex-SAS man who seeks revenge for a 'too professional' hit-and-run on his daughter. Rebus will play unfair in order to bring the criminal to justice – his personal version of justice – but one has to be careful what one wishes for when looking for justice...

The Hanging Garden succeeds on many levels. To begin with it's a strong, gritty story about the power struggle between gangs. It's also about the tolerance level between the Police Force and organised crime. Then it's about John Rebus, who cuts through all that bullshit to get at the criminals he wants but tries desperately to protect his vast assortment of women – estranged friendships – at the same time; it would be comical if not so bloody sad.

I'm making Rebus sound like Dirty Harry here, but he

doesn't need a 44 Magnum – he's got his bare hands and perceptive mind to pin his victim to the wall. No bullets are required. He's a tough, broad, middle-aged man with a lot of baggage but somehow he gets the job done, albeit not in the most considered way.

The Hanging Garden takes on other dark themes too, such as refugee prostitution and consequently racialism on a wide scale. It brings the north of England – Newcastle – together with Scotland's capital city in order to show the scope of the criminal underworld's networking scene and just what depth of corruption the Police Force have to deal with. But Rebus is prepared to meet that corruption head on, if only to take his revenge on the person who hurt his daughter.

He explains to a colleague that there is no line to cross when doing his duty. This probably explains why he is so poor in personal relationships: Rebus is too good at his job to have a deep and meaningful relationship and this is clearly illustrated in *The Hanging Garden*. Once he breaks a suspect down and follows up another lead, his day is already overlong. So he calls his already estranged girlfriend, Patience, to ask how late he is permitted to be before she disowns him once more! He gets deeply embroiled in the characters that conspire against each other – and him. When Telford – a rival of Cafferty – tells Rebus to get in a car because he wants to show him something, Rebus, 'world's craziest cop', does. That's where he steps over the invisible line between the good guys and bad. He's not afraid of the baddies, he knows they wouldn't do anything stupid – and there lies a mutual respect.

Rebus pin-balls between Telford and Cafferty in *The*

Hanging Garden and he is happy to do so: he needs to know who is lying to him and who is telling him the truth. Rebus sets things in motion by leaving his desk and making things happen. He then drops into the unfolding events to analyse and solve the case. In that respect he is a little like Sherlock Holmes with Siobhan as his ever-astute but still-marvelling sidekick. It's only towards the end that all the ends get tied together and the truth becomes clear. Some could argue that that is a little too neat but let us remember that wasn't necessarily the outcome of either *Let It Bleed* or *Black and Blue*.

All of this really showed how far away from his creator Rebus had grown.

The Hanging Garden was really the first book Rankin wrote as a bestselling writer and he really delivered a no-holds-barred story that worked on different moral levels. The theme of exploitation of Eastern European women in international prostitution was played against the search for ex-Nazis and the truth behind the Rat Run (the exodus of Nazis from Germany at the conclusion of the war via underground tunnels). Moral dilemmas, racialism, exploitation, the corruption of groups – gangs, political parties – and individuals are all part of the jigsaw of evil that Rankin explores in *The Hanging Garden*, but he never over-eggs it. He unfolds each layer carefully until he is prepared to bring in his satisfying conclusion.

But with *The Hanging Garden*, Rankin's conclusion harks back to the book's opening quote from T S Eliot: 'If all time is eternally present, all time is unredeemable.' It was General Patton who was convinced that in order to win a war you had to study history and see where the current conflict was repeating itself and then learn by history's mistakes. What Rankin – T S Eliot – tells us is that the same or similar things will happen time and again and the outcome will be different enough to be repeated throughout the whole of future history. History is a self-replicating process that has as many repeat performances as any given Shakespearean play. And like Shakespearian plays the world remembers war. In his Afterword to *The Hanging Garden*, Rankin stated that a Nazi-inflicted extermination of a whole village depicted in the story actually happened. It was Saturday 10 June 1944 that 3rd Company, Das Reich, killed up to one thousand people in Oradour-sur-Glane in France, and Oradour still stands as a shrine. 'The village has been left just the way it was on that day in June 1944,' Rankin said.

Right at the end of the book Rankin reminds the reader of the racial issues tackled in the book. He shows disgust at the 12,000 foreign volunteers of the Waffen SS who were still receiving pensions from the Federal German government in 1998 and marvelling why nobody was really held accountable for the holocaust at Oradour. Perhaps that is one aspect of his time in France that wasn't so pleasant to learn about, but he made a point of highlighting it, Rebus-style, when he got the chance.

> '… who would bare the whips and scorns of time,
> The oppressors wrong, the proud man's contumely,
> The pangs of despis'd love, the law's delay,
> The insolence of office… The undiscovered country,
> From whose bourn no traveler returns…'
>
> William Shakespeare, *Hamlet*

CHAPTER FIFTEEN

WRITING IN REALITY

ankin has always stated that Rebus lives in real time, so there was always a time bomb ticking towards his natural retirement, which the author couldn't do anything about. That said, Rankin explained that fans had come up with many ways in which the series could continue after the inevitable retirement: Rebus could unofficially assist Siobhan, or Rankin could go back to Rebus's early cases, i.e. those that occurred before *Knots and Crosses,* and write about them.

When Rankin was winding Rebus down he didn't want to consider any of the above options. The copper had to retire and that was the reality of the situation – just as in real life. And it is this association with reality that brings credibility – inevitability – to the series. Everything, after all, must come to an end. However, a line from *The Hanging Garden* does give interesting pause for thought. When Rebus has written an account of his whereabouts over the past 24 hours, it is stated: 'Back at his desk, he started on his memoirs...'

Surely in retirement the methodical Detective Inspector could make some sense – justification for his own piece of mind – by writing his memoirs? It could probably allow Rankin to re-write one of his previous Rebus books from Rebus's point of view – and have a completely different outcome! It would also allow Rankin to explore the character's army days and formative time on the Police Force. But maybe there is cold comfort from the fact that we know Rebus did the best job he could and that is the final epitaph – the only epitaph – that anyone is left with when contemplating their prime and the work they did throughout their lifetime.

> 'They learned what troubles in her career Miss Brodie had encountered on their behalf. "It is for the sake of you girls – my influence, now, in the years of my prime." This was the beginning of the Brodie set.'
>
> Muriel Spark, *The Prime of Miss Jean Brodie*

There is a similarity in philosophy of life between Rankin's work and that of Spark. Clearly, something would have rubbed off on Rankin after studying the authoress's work at university. But there is something more: that familiarity with Edinburgh past, from Deacon Brodie to the works of Robert Louis Stevenson. It's almost as if Rankin has taken the Brodie set — that little clique of like-minded people — one step further and into the 21st century.

In a *Book and Magazine Collector* interview (issue 221), Rankin mentioned a whole bunch of Scottish writers as influences, or important to Scottish literature. You won't find him talking too much about Charles Dickens and William Shakespeare: frankly, there are too many people who could do this. No, Rankin wants to explore his own country's talent, and he is right to do so. As Bono would joyously shout out at Slane Castle 'This is our tribe!' there is the same level of pride when Ian Rankin gives away copies of Robert Louis Stevenson's *Kidnapped* to the youth of Edinburgh to try and encourage them to read more. And like every U2 fan who wants to experience Ireland through their favourite band's music, Rankin allows you to explore the real Scotland through its/his fiction.

When Arthur Freed, producer of *Brigadoon*, stated, 'I went to Scotland and found nothing there that looks like Scotland,' he was expecting only the shortbread-tin pictures that make up a tiny piece of the history and character of the country. More importantly, he didn't get to grips with the psyche of the place, its people today and their so ordinary lives.

And that's why Rebus lived in real time: to remind the world that unfulfilment and disillusionment are fundamental parts of everyday life on the council estates around the inner bubble of Edinburgh. If you really want to explore the underbelly of Scottish society, wander in to a youth club or job centre and count how many kilts and bagpipes you find.

"'… Depend on it, the advice of the great preacher is genuine: 'What thine hand findeth to do, do it with thy might, for none of us knows what a day may bring forth?' That is, none of us knows what is pre-ordained, but whatever is pre-ordained we must do, and none of these things will be laid to our charge.'"

James Hogg, *The Private Memoirs and Confessions of a Justified Sinner*

Rankin and Rebus have aged together. Rebus is approximately 15 years senior to his creator but they have both lived through the same technological advances (within the Police Force) and that keeps us looking at the comparisons between creator and creation. However, as both get older, they appear to drift further away from each other too…

Ian Rankin,
August 2009.
© Rex Features

Above: Craig Cabell and Ian Rankin in conversation at the 2010 London Book Fair.

© *Nathan Cabel*

Below: These wooden dolls, found at Arthur's Seat in the 19th Century provided inspiration for Rankin's novel *The Falls*, one of the very best Rebus titles.

The Home of
ROBERT LOUIS STEVENSON
1857 – 1880

17 Heriot Row, the former Edinburgh home of Robert Louis Stevenson.

Above left: Ian Rankin, around the time he wrote *The Black Book*.

©Miranda Harve

Above right: The first edition of the first Inspector Rebus novel, *Knots and Crosses*.

Below left: The first proof copy of *Hide and Seek*, the second Rebus novel.

Below right: Publicity material and an advance copy of *Fleshmarket Close*.

A view of Edinburgh (above) taken from the Castle (below).

Left: The Oxford Bar, Inspector Rebus' favourite pub

Below: Mary King's Close, the setting of the seven pack murder in *Mortal Causes*.

Bottom: Welcome to Fleshmarket Close!

n Fleshmarket Close in Edinburgh during National Braille Week,
), launching an appeal to help re-house the Edinburgh-based
lle Press. © *Andrew Milligan/PA Wire*

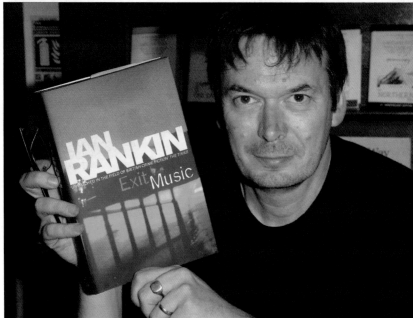

Above: Rankin comes face to face with one of his youngest fans.

Below: Promoting *Exit Music*, billed as the concluding book in the Inspector Rebus series.

CHAPTER SIXTEEN

JIGSAW PUZZLE

'My life has been a life of trouble and turmoil;
of change and vicissitude; of anger and exultation; of
sorrow and of vengeance. My sorrows have all been
for a slighted gospel, and my vengeance has been
wreaked on its adversaries.'

James Hogg, *The Private Memoirs and Confessions of a Justified Sinner*

When one reads the basic story for *Set in Darkness*, one marvels at how such a bizarre story is made plausible. Rebus and DI Derek Linford are seconded to the police liaison team for the new Scottish parliament. Rebus senses that 'Farmer' Watson is behind all this – yet again – but the Farmer isn't without his justification. Linford is by-the-book from the off, while Rebus is his usual off-the-wall self and this clearly means that Rebus's patience will be severely tested before they even start. A corpse is found behind a fireplace in a parliament building. Suddenly Roddy Grieve, Labour MP, is found dead and, bizarrely, Rebus begins to suspect there is a connection between Grieve's murder and the body in the fireplace. Add Siobhan Clarke witnessing the suicide of a homeless man who just happens to have

£400,000 in the bank in the same name as the corpse in the fireplace and you have the interlocking story from hell. And then 'Big Ger' is released from prison and things get even more involved.

Yes, I'm being slightly flippant but not without good cause. As we know, every novel from *Let It Bleed/Black and Blue* onwards has a series of threads that are all entwined to make a bigger picture of Edinburgh's intricate life-in-crime, and *Set in Darkness* is no exception.

The story is made more credible when one learns of the bizarre chain of serendipity that led to the writing of it. Rankin was flying between cities during a publicity tour in America. While on the plane he picked up the in-flight magazine and found an article about walking tours in Edinburgh. Thinking that he knew all that there was to know about such things, he was surprised to learn about Queensberry House, where there is a grisly legend about the master of the house spit-roasting and eating one of the servants (later bricking up the remains in the fireplace).

When back in Edinburgh, Rankin decided to check out the building, taking along a film crew who were keen to find out how Rankin constructed storylines for his Rebus series. Once at the house, which was part of the new parliament complex, Rankin found to his amazement some archaeologists who had just excavated the old kitchen, which had a big metal facade in front of it. Rankin asked for the doorway to be opened, which it was, but no old corpse lay anywhere behind it. But that's not to say that he couldn't invent a complex story based around the legend.

OK, so we can see where the idea came from but, more

so, we can clearly see where Rankin's 'obsessive' need to find the full story of an historic snippet of Edinburgh's past comes from. He explores – investigates – in a similar way to Rebus himself: pulling the threads together, visiting the sights, meeting the locals – the people working in the building – until he makes the ultimate discovery. (Note: he was the one who asked for the ancient seal to be opened and then the first to glimpse inside.) Rankin's thirst for the story is as keen as a journalist looking for their scoop. And here lies a very important observation regarding Ian Rankin and Inspector Rebus: the way Rebus follows a path of inquiry is the same as way as his creator. Indeed, before he was aware of how the police carried out their investigations, Rankin followed what he thought was a logical path of inquiry for Rebus. He later found that he wasn't far wrong with his assumptions.

So the methodical way of investigating 'stories' became Rebus's police procedure? Absolutely, and when the red-tape of police logging/reporting, etc. etc. came in, Rankin just ignored the whole thing and made Rebus a maverick, conducting his investigations in the same manner as the ordinary man on the street might examine something that interested him.

So if Rankin is actually his creation Rebus, does that mean Rankin is a maverick too? Well, what is a maverick? Someone who refuses to play by the rules; someone who isn't scared to cross the line of conformity.

Have we just described Rankin? Many would say no. Rankin is the academic wordsmith who searches Edinburgh and Scottish literature for interesting stories and legends and creates something of a legend with his maverick cop John Rebus. But is that just the kindly Dr Jekyll side of Ian Rankin? Is Mr Hyde moving in and out of the darkness behind that pleasant exterior? Don't forget, Rebus followed the normal career path of a boy from Cardenden, not Rankin. Rankin followed his dream of becoming a novelist, flying in the face of the academic world he was plunged into at university. Every step of the way, he isn't doing things by the book. He is slightly left of field each time. And would you say writing a bestselling series of books about a Scottish cop is the norm? No, it isn't. It breaks the mould, it rewrites the annals of crime fiction, it makes us look again at the great crime novels and see where Rebus — that multifaceted picture-puzzle of a man — comes from. And the answer is simple: from the natural instincts of the man who created him, Ian Rankin.

> '"Maybe," Rebus replied, putting the bottle back to his mouth.'
>
> *Set in Darkness*

Something that interests me deeply about Ian Rankin is his big watershed novel *Black and Blue*. For whatever reason, Rankin was more cavalier in his approach to Rebus during that book. He bounced him around Scotland, forcing him to experience many things and seeing how the DI coped with it. Rankin was under a lot of pressure in his life at the time and just for a change, he took an extra risk, pushed the envelope a little further and found the bestselling formula — the blueprint — that would shape the rest of the series.

IAN RANKIN AND INSPECTOR REBUS

My opinion is that Rankin is a bit of a reluctant maverick – a shy Mr Hyde if you will. At heart he is a sensible man, but every now and then he forces himself to make a change. In the Rebus series we first notice this with *The Black Book* and that 'closer to reality' way of writing (as well as the introduction of what would become two major characters). Then there was *Black and Blue*. So was *Set in Darkness* the next major step? No, not quite. It was the stepping stone that led to it though, and that book was *The Falls* – a book where Rebus has his first real taste of mortality against the youngsters and where we begin to like him more.

CHAPTER SEVENTEEN

MIDNIGHT RAMBLER

'The retirement party for Detective
Chief Superintendent 'Farmer' Watson
had commenced at six.'
The Falls

Before we move on to *The Falls*, there is a very important thing that we've just highlighted: the breakthrough novels in the series — the ones that have become benchmarks along the way, taking the author and character to new heights. Rankin considers *Strip Jack* to be the first of those, then perhaps *Let It Bleed* with its introduction of the three-pronged plotlines. Then there is *Set in Darkness*? The interesting thing is, the novels that follow all of these are the ones that truly make the difference: *The Black Book*, *Black and Blue* and *The Falls*, then later *Fleshmarket Close* and *The Naming of the Dead*.

Rankin enjoys tackling themes but not necessarily pushing the boundaries. So he manages to do it by default. The decisions to use real-life locations and pubs in *The Black*

Book with the new characters was the first big break, then the refinement of the three-pronged plotlines and real-life case in *Black and Blue*, followed by a true, open-ended, macabre Edinburgh story…

> 'The wind howled chilly and with a mournful cadence through the funnel-like closes, up the winding high street and round the castle rock, raising wavelets on the dull Nor' Loch and shaking from the creaking trees such withered leaves as autumn had not taken long before.'
>
> Robert Louis Stevenson, *The Plague-Cellar*

We've discovered that the dark, gothic history of Edinburgh is the strong backbone to Rankin's work. All of this would culminate after Rebus's final novel in the series, *Exit Music*, with his first – 'and last' – graphic novel, the Gaiman-like *Dark Entries* (Vertigo, 2009). *Dark Entries* was a horror/fairy tale that Rankin said took him 'full circle', as he started out writing comic books as a child. It was also proof of Rankin's fascination with the macabre, which is highlighted strongly in the Rebus series.[lvii]

One of the finest boogie tales in the series is *The Falls*. It ranks alongside *Mortal Causes* and *Fleshmarket Close* in its ability to mix the history of Edinburgh, the unseen present-day city, and a hint of fairy-tale darkness.

'Like a lot of my stories, *The Falls* started with a bit of serendipity,' Rankin explained. 'Around the time of the

---

lvii Author interview 20 August 2009.

opening of the Scottish parliament, there was some international media interest. There was a French TV crew in Edinburgh. They wanted to interview me and ask me a few questions about the parliament. I agreed and they suggested that we do the interview in the new Museum of Scotland, which had recently opened. When I got there, a curator was waiting to take us up to the place where we could film, and he said to me, "You should write something about the Arthur's Seat dolls," Now Arthur's Seat is a big hill in Edinburgh and I can see it from my front window, but I told the curator that I had never heard of the dolls. He went on to tell me that they were on the fourth floor of the museum and I should go and see them, but I didn't get a chance that day. I did the interview and went back home.

'It started to niggle me. I thought, I don't know what he's talking about, so I went back to the museum a few weeks later and found the dolls. There are about seven or eight of them left but there were originally 17. They are wooden dolls, four to five inches long, dressed in clothes and inside well-made, tiny wooden coffins. They were found in a cave at Arthur's Seat by some kids in 1836 and of course nobody knows what they were doing there.

'Now during the whole series of books I've been trying to talk about the hidden Edinburgh, the Edinburgh the tourist never sees, but here was a bit of Edinburgh I didn't even know about and a beautiful, open-ended mystery, which I could use as a storyline.

'All of this happened some time ago and it just sat in the back of my mind until I worked out how I could use it. And then I got the idea of a girl being abducted, a little coffin being found in the present day and, to solve that crime, Rebus had to go back and solve the original crime, or at least give some explanation as to why the dolls had been left there.'[lviii]

The story of the dolls was perfect and reminded Rankin of another piece of serendipity that had occurred with the writing of one of his previous books in the series, *The Hanging Garden*: 'When I was living in France I went to a place called Oradour-sur-Glane. It was a place where a real-life atrocity was carried out by the 3rd Company of the SS Das Reich regiment. It was about 40 or 50 miles away from where I was living and the village has been kept exactly the same since the atrocity occurred. An entire village. A thousand people. There is a stationary tram and then the church where the Germans killed all the women and children. There are bullet holes in the walls and it is such a powerful place. I felt such a feeling of injustice because nobody went there and nobody was brought to justice.

'Well, the problem was how could I [incorporate] that in a novel set in modern-day Edinburgh. And it took me two or three years and then suddenly I thought, Wait a moment – what if there was an alleged Nazi war criminal in Edinburgh, and Rebus is alerted to this and has to decide a) is it the guy and b) if it is, is it worth prosecuting? And it brought in all kinds of moral questions. Then I moved back from France and found that there was an alleged Nazi war criminal living in Edinburgh, who was extradited to

lviii Author interview March 2001.

Lithuania to stand trial for his crimes – serendipity, as I told you!'[lix] And a touch of Frederick Forsyth too maybe (a la *Odessa File*), but the story is a good example of how a true story can wait for discovery and then have a relevance and impact on modern-day events and people.[lx]

Rankin is very focused on the here and now and the technological advance of the world appertaining to the Police Force. As I mentioned earlier, the Rebus series was written in real time across a 20-year period when many technological advances were made, and this gives the series an added importance.

'The internet is potentially a very dark force because there are no barriers, no moral guardians and, when you have children keen to go on the net, how far can you control that? And the thing about the internet game came up [*The Falls*], because there was a story I read a few years ago about a French student who was mad keen on Sword and Sorcery, Dungeons and Dragons and the internet. And he was found dead on a Scottish hillside. Just a body found. Desiccated, because it had been up there so long. And there was a gun found a couple of yards away, so the police concluded that the person had committed suicide and thrown the gun away as he shot himself in the head! But the parents found that it was their son eventually and one of the theories expounded at the time was that he somehow got involved in some very

---

lix Author interview March 2001.

lx Rankin has told me (author interview 5 November 2004) that Frederick Forsyth 'was an inspiration to me when I was a teenager – reading his thrillers and hoping I might even write my own one day.' Something Rankin did as Jack Harvey and much earlier with *Watchman*.

dark and devious internet role-playing game, which led to the Scottish hillside where somebody killed him off. It never went any further than that; but it came back in my mind as an intriguing possibility.

'So the story inspired something that Rebus had no conception of and I wanted that. Rebus is in his fifties. He's never been to university, he came straight out of the army and into the police and is now up against all the younger officers who are completely internet friendly, because that is the way the police are going nowadays. They see the internet as a tool, which gathers more and more information that used to be stored by card index.'[lxi]

The Falls was a perfect opportunity for Siobhan Clarke to prove herself, for she could lead the virtual investigation.

'Putting together a misfit team from the Lothian and Borders finest, Rebus takes the unpromising historical material and runs with it, leaving DC Siobhan Clarke to take her chances with the virtual Quizmaster. She's young enough to know how to navigate the net, but is she old enough and wise enough to pick up the clues in such a complex case?'

The above is dustwrapper blurb for *The Falls* but it does encapsulate what was going on with the characters in the story. Suddenly Rebus wasn't solving cases single-handedly. Rebus was being overtaken by events. New toys and new blood were coming in and suddenly he experiences more of an uphill struggle when completing his day-to-day inquiries and – this is another reason why *The Falls* is such a milestone

lxi Author interview March 2001.

novel in the series – it is the first book where Rebus begins to show his age.

In 2001, Rankin told me: 'The police have HOLMES, which is the Home Office Large Major Enquiry System. It is a software tool and, when there is a huge inquiry going on, it can find links between somebody who was interviewed six months ago and somebody who was interviewed last week about the same thing. So the system finds links between things you might miss.'[lxii]

So age suddenly becomes an issue and consequently this is where Rankin spiritually moves even further away from Rebus and begins to identify more with Siobhan. This isn't really something new. We should have seen it coming in *Mortal Causes*:

> 'So they [Clarke and Rebus] sat at Millie's desk, like customers and assistant. Clarke, who liked computers, had actually picked up a couple of brochures.
> "That's got a twenty-five megahertz micro-processor," Millie said, pointing to one of the brochures.
> "What size memory?"'

Where Siobhan wins over a witness through a mutual interest in computers, Rebus sits on the touchline feeling the chill beginning to settle in.

Siobhan is suddenly the star of the show, most definitely

---

lxii Author interview March 2001.

in the novel that followed *The Falls*: *Resurrection Men*.

So what is left for Rebus? Frustration. In *Resurrection Men* Rebus loses his temper with Gill Templer (again!) and is sent to the Scottish Police College for retraining.

Resurrection Men was written quickly after *The Falls*, and the book was already in progress during *The Falls* publicity campaign, as Rankin told me at the time: 'In the next book he's going to police college. I know that because I've just started writing it. And he gets [knowing laugh, as if giving too much away], he gets kicked off a case for insubordination and sent back to college with a bunch of reprobates who are in their last chance saloon. And if they – and Rebus – don't discover how to work as a team again – become team players – they're going to get kicked off the force. So it's a kind of Dirty Dozen operation.'[lxiii]

Resurrection Men was an important title in the series, as it made clear that Rebus was being labelled a dinosaur and consequently left behind. It's not just the fact that Rebus finds himself in his last chance saloon – Siobhan Clarke, his understudy, has been promoted and is coming more into her own, developing the case Rebus was taken off after his outburst against Templer. It seems that the world is moving on but John Rebus isn't. In that regard *Resurrection Men* is a book about life's rich career path and how the older officer is overshadowed by the thrusting young junior, full of good ideas and energy.

It is normally at this stage that the older officer becomes the sober voice of experience and grows old graciously. (As

lxiii Author interview March 2001.

The Rolling Stones would observe, it's a drag getting old!) Well, that wasn't really going to happen with John Rebus, was it? Especially the 'sober' bit! But the voice of experience is in him, like it or not. As he goes through the unsolved cases given to him at college, he suddenly recognises one of the victims, Rico Lomax, a Glasgow thug who had few friends. Suddenly the whole college thing takes a macabre turn and when things couldn't get more complex for Rebus, 'Big Ger' Cafferty is released from Barlinnie.

The final outcome is brought to a satisfying conclusion by Rebus using all his experience to solve the varied threads of the case(s) and working as part of a team with the young blood – the newly promoted Siobhan Clarke. It's at this juncture that the two find a strong connection, not sexual, but an important bond that assists their ongoing career in the Police Force. Siobhan can learn from Rebus's experience, maverick or not, while he will be helped with all the technology stuff and red tape. Ah, it's a perfect match and perhaps a politically correct, modern-day Holmes and Watson as well!

Rankin told me that he 'made all the cases up' in *Resurrection Men*. 'In my previous half dozen books I've used real-life unsolved mysteries as the kick-off point.'[lxiv]

So was Rankin going back to his old style of total invention? 'I do have to check things out,' he said. 'Two of my neighbours are lawyers and I go to them when I have any problems or queries… I have consulted advocates, and once attended a party given by a top law officer in Scotland,

---

lxiv Author interview March 2002.

where I got to talk with judges, one of whom gave me his business card in case I ever needed to ask him anything.'[lxv]

No. The world had moved on for Rankin and Rebus. The books had become more effortless but not less satisfying, as the next four novels – the final four novels in the series – would testify.

> 'We all get things we feel we don't deserve...
> Most of us treat them as windfalls. Your career so
> far has been a success. Is that the problem perhaps?
> You don't want that easy success? You want to be
> an outsider, someone who breaks the rules with
> only a measure of impunity?' she paused. 'Maybe
> you want to be like DI Rebus?'
>
> *Resurrection Men*

---

lxv Author interview March 2002.

CHAPTER EIGHTEEN

THE YOUNGSTER COMES OF AGE

'At the moment, Siobhan is staying just this side of the
angels – she wants promotion after all, and knows
there's only room in the force for one maverick. She
plays a clever game. I think she'll go far.' [lxvi]

Ian Rankin

So let us discuss Siobhan Clarke for a moment. What has
been her role? Throughout the Rebus novels she has
played a greater part and with *A Question of Blood*, she really
gets the upper hand on Rebus after he literally burns his
fingers. But what is Siobhan's relationship with Rebus? Is it
totally platonic? Totally professional? Or is there a degree of
sexual tension? During the *A Question of Blood* promotional
round, I asked Rankin these questions.

'Siobhan has been called my insurance policy,' he said,
'because she is getting more to do in each book and in this
new book I give her a position of physical power over Rebus
because he gets his fingers badly burnt and she has to do

---

lxvi Author Interview March 2002.

everything for him, or *nearly* everything… I wanted her to refuse to light his cigarettes, for example! So he has to get strangers in the street to light his cigarettes for him. I liked the idea of him being in her power. Good doing the research for that actually: I went wandering around my house with my hands heavily bandaged. I tried to pick up a cup, make a telephone call. Could I open doors? Then somebody asked, "Can you pee?" and I thought, Oh, I never thought of that and disappeared again… it all comes across in the book!

'But she [Siobhan] is a good example of a very minor character, just another colleague who helps in the police station, coming to the fore. Very quickly I found her absolutely fascinating, basically because she is a woman in a man's world. The police in Scotland, especially CID, are very male-orientated.'[lxvii]

A similar thing struck me and while reading *A Question of Blood*, I actually queried Siobhan's sexuality. I put this to Rankin, who pondered for a moment. 'Na, I don't think she's bisexual. I thought about her sexuality quite a lot. To begin with I thought about putting her and Rebus in a clinch, but that would be the obvious thing to do, because the two of them *could* get together as they are quite similar in many ways. Then I thought, no, that's kind of a middle-aged man's fantasy, isn't it? She's half his age. So it's much more avuncular: he's more like her uncle. Near the end of the book there is a clinch, which leaves things a little open, and people will wonder what will happen next? But I don't think anything will!

---

lxvii Author interview 27 August 2003.

'I have wondered if she's lesbian, bisexual, I don't know. I don't think it really matters that much. She's had some pretty bad relationships with men in the past: she chooses her blokes very badly. They turn out to be stalkers and criminal masterminds!'

But in 2003, was Rankin grooming Siobhan to take over from Rebus?

'I do think she has got it within her to carry a series now, and I do feel fairly comfortable writing from her point of view. In the early books there weren't many female characters, because I didn't think I could do it. It was really only when female cops started saying that they liked Siobhan and Gill Templer and the situations I put them in. I was surprised and thought, All right, I'll do a bit more of that then. And I can't think of one male writer who runs a series of books with a female lead. Plenty of women do it but not men.'

So Rankin was keeping his options open regarding Siobhan Clarke and still is. 'By the time of *Naming of the Dead* I knew Rebus was on his way out – 60 was approaching,' he told me in July 2009. I was wondering how Siobhan would feel about this, and maybe I was sizing her up as a protagonist who could carry the series without her one-time mentor. Jury's still out on that…'

A Question of Blood dealt with some really big issues, such as child abuse, and Dunblane, and in that respect it is probably the darkest novel from a social issues point of view. It is as hard and fast as a 1960s TV play. Rankin comments: 'I think it all connects. I think that's the thing with the Rebus series:

it works on the assumption that a butterfly flaps its wings in South America and there's a tornado in Europe. The way a small community deals with a big tragedy, whether it be Lockerbie or Dunblane or wherever, that fascinated me, because suddenly they have all these strangers coming into their world, cops and media. The locals don't want them there but they're inextricably linked to what has happened. So I wanted to look at that, I wanted to look at the families involved, the victims, which is why the killing has already happened at the beginning of the book. I wasn't interested in that per se: I was more interested in the aftermath.

'The book is full of outsiders, absolutely chock-a-block, whether it's Rebus who is the perennial outsider – the ex-SAS guy who hasn't quite fitted back into society – or it's teenagers who refuse to come out of their bedrooms and only have relationships with people on the internet. Everybody is cut away from everybody else and there are small communities who are breaking up because of this, because of that lack of interaction. They prefer to send somebody a text message, sit in front of a TV or computer and we're all getting very isolated, so *A Question of Blood* is a book about isolation. And the opposite of that is family ties, which is why I introduce one of Rebus's cousins as one of the victims. And that's interesting because Rebus has completely thrown his family away; he hasn't seen them for decades. And when it comes to it, they are still there and there are still memories, but where Rebus thought that they were close, it turns out that they really weren't at all. The memory can lie.'[lxviii]

[lxviii] Author interview 27 August 2003.

A Question of Blood opens with a shooting at a private school. Two 17-year-olds are killed by an ex-Army loner who has gone off the rails. On the surface there is little to investigate as the loner turned the gun on himself after killing the teenagers, but Rebus and Siobhan find themselves investigating more than the 'why?' of the case. There are personal issues/connections for Rebus: Army and family...

'With this book I was very interested in people coming back from the first Gulf War,' Rankin told me. 'There were a lot of stories about mainly American squaddies coming back and suddenly not being able to cope with their family life and turning to violence. There was a lot of violence against wives, there were a lot of murders of spouses and a few suicides, and at the same time there had been a few high-profile suicides in the British ex-forces. For example, the guy who took off in a light aeroplane and jumped out – he had written a book called *Free Fall*, which was about the crack-up he had after leaving the SAS. He tried to kill his wife at one time, he tried to commit suicide, he got into drugs.

'I've always been interested by the outsider, the person who doesn't fit back in to [a conventional lifestyle]. You can't really leave behind the forces. It doesn't matter if you're just an electrician in the RAF or you're a trained killer in the SAS – when you leave and go back onto civvy street, you don't just switch off. You've still got a lot of that mentality, that training, a certain amount of baggage you carry around with you. It's difficult to switch off. And the Army investigators in the book have flagged up Rebus as a potential time bomb because he screwed up big time when he was training for the SAS. And now he's gone into a stressed job with violent confrontations from time to time, so they're expecting him to go off the deep end. He's looking into the suicide of a guy and the investigators are looking into him! It's wheels within wheels.

'Once you start a story, you think it's quite a small intimate story, but then you say, "Oh, this will be interesting". When I started plotting the book, I had no idea the Army investigators would come into it until I started plotting it out. It was then that I thought that the Army would send somebody along; it wouldn't just be the Police Force. And bringing them in and creating Rebus's mistrust of them added a whole new dimension to the story, which wasn't there when it was dreamed up!

'I think Rebus joined the Police Force because it allowed him to be a voyeur – it allowed him to look into other people's lives rather than look into his own. So it's a way of him warding off his own problems… But somebody who is well balanced and spends their life doing the right thing isn't very interesting to read about! We're into villains; the good guys aren't that interesting. Is there such a thing as evil? Or are people just misguided, or chemically imbalanced? What I try to do with a book is put the reader in the situation where they say, "Shit, would I do that?" How far would you go to protect your kids? Would you commit murder? Would you go off the rails? How far could you go off the rails? I think the best crime fiction right now is asking very big questions about the world we live in. I think the literary novel is almost totally ignoring major issues;

they're backward-looking books, almost historical. They're not looking at the here and now.'

There are many serious issues in *A Question of Blood*. I was interested to learn where the story really started for Rankin. 'The thing that kicked this book off was a woman who asked me at an event [*Resurrection Men* promotion], "Mr Rankin, why do you never write about private schools?" Now there are tons of private schools in Edinburgh and I didn't have a Scooby what they were like, so I found out. And that was the first nugget that started the book. And all through the year I collect little bits of news, put them in a big folder and come October I look through them and see what interests me and where I can take it. And between now and then, somebody could come up to me in a pub and tell me a good story and suddenly I'm away again. But that's how it happened for *A Question of Blood*.'[lxix]

To me, Siobhan Clarke and the story content seemed more important to Rankin this time round. Rebus is almost treated in a comic way with his damaged fingers. And what is important to us for this book, it seems again that Rebus was moving further away from his creator and Rankin's energy was being poured more into Siobhan Clarke, the person he seems to – at this stage – empathise with more.

> '"Siobhan!" he yelled. She raised a hand, waved it… And was picked off the ground by Rebus, his hug enveloping her.

---

lxix Author interview 27 August 2003.

"Ow, ow, ow," she said, causing him to ease off. "Bit bruised," she explained, her eyes meeting his. He couldn't help himself, planted his lips on hers. The kiss lingered…'

A Question of Blood

CHAPTER NINETEEN

REBUS AND HIS NEMESIS GET OLD

'Rebus's eyes narrowed. "You know
something, don't you?"
"Not me, Rebus... I'm happy just sitting here
and growing old."'

Fleshmarket Close

Fleshmarket Close continued the thread of big issues started
with *A Question of Blood*. Illegal immigrants, racial attacks,
rape and two skeletons — a woman and an infant — found
buried beneath a concrete cellar in Fleshmarket Close!

It is quite apparent that Rankin wanted to tackle ever
bigger themes in his novels. During my *A Question of Blood*
interview, he called himself 'a political writer' and he
probably adopted that style to an increasing extent from
around *Let It Bleed/Black and Blue*, becoming stronger and
stronger and peaking with *A Question of Blood*, *Fleshmarket
Close* and *The Naming of the Dead*. No longer did Rebus have
anything to do with Rankin, other than a love of 'spit and
sawdust pubs', something Rankin expanded upon in my
Fleshmarket Close interview.

'There's one scene in the book where Rebus takes a girlfriend to The Oxford Bar, because she has insisted on seeing what it is like, because she thinks she can tell what he is like from what his local is like. And when they get there, Siobhan is there and Rebus is mortified because Siobhan has taken over the bar. She is the one with all the people around her, she's the one making people laugh and doing all the chatting, and that's his job, it's his bar. There's a lot of tension in that scene, because he's pitched up with a girlfriend and Siobhan doesn't like the idea that he has a girlfriend and he doesn't like the fact that she is in his pub.'[lxx]

All of this happens not because Siobhan fancies Rebus, but because Rebus's girlfriend is an outsider. The police go around in little gangs and suddenly a woman comes in who is not part of the group and that's why Siobhan doesn't like her.

Another hurdle Rebus – and ostensibly Rankin – had to face in *Fleshmarket Close* was leaving St Leonard's. In real life, St Leonard's ceased to have a CID unit in 2003. Rankin found this out during his promotion round for *A Question of Blood* and told me at the time that he had received a text from a policeman of his acquaintance who told him about it, so instantly that had to be worked into the next novel. This allowed the prospect of retirement to raise its head but despite his trusty sidekick outplaying him in his local bar and the many other jokes that hit Rebus since at least *Resurrection Men* (being sent to boot camp, having his fingers burned – things that provoked laughter and/or ridicule), he stuck tenaciously to the cases that came to his desk like a

lxx Author interview 22 September 2004.

barnacle to the underside of an ancient barge. His tenaciousness, his single-minded determination throughout, smacks of that displayed by his creator: the single-mindedness to become a writer in the first place, the tenaciousness, the never-say-die attitude, and the quality of the writing of the series – especially during the early days – when Rankin had to do other jobs to subsidise his living.

So although there was little to make comparisons of between Rebus and Rankin in the text, the overall mind-set was still there. Maybe that's endemic in all writers and their creations: fiction is dictated by the personality of the writer. Where an Oscar Wilde character will stop in the park and smell a rose on the way to work, a Rankin character will stop off at the local pub. Some of the genetic make-up will rub off. Taking this analogy further, it is strange how many siblings who haven't seen each other since childhood grow up and follow similar career paths, or make the same decisions with regard to relationships – it's in their genetic make-up.

With *Fleshmarket Close*, Rebus is feeling his age somewhat. To a degree this is forced upon him as he enters the new police station at Gayfield Square:

> 'I'm one of the lucky ones, Detective Sergeant Clarke was thinking to herself, by which she meant that she at least had been given a desk of her own. John Rebus – senior in rank to her – hadn't been so fortunate. Not that fortune, good or bad, had had anything to do with it. She knew Rebus saw it as a sign from on high: we've no place for you; time you thought of chucking it in.'

Rebus doesn't let the buggers grind him down and tells Siobhan on the phone that he quite likes the new station really, especially when everyone has gone home, because he can have any desk he wants! The workaholic in Rebus wins through, but the retirement issue comes up again through his taste in music. His new batch of CDs include Jackie Leven, Lou Reed and John Mayall's Bluesbreakers, while Siobhan's choice includes the sprightly Snow Patrol and Grant-Lee Philips!

Another interesting scene is where Rebus turns up at Cafferty's house, a large detached house on a dimly lit suburban street. Cafferty has an outside jacuzzi and although it is quite late, he is still lounging in it, listening to music, without a care in the world. Although Rebus doesn't admit it, he must be jealous. He is roughly the same age as Cafferty, has worked hard on the right side of the law, even put this gangster away, but here he is with more creature comforts than he damn well deserves and, just to rub it in, he tells Rebus: 'I love it out here, this time of night. Hear the wind in the trees, Rebus? They've been here longer than any of us, those trees. Same with these houses. And they'll still be here when we've gone.' Cafferty is enjoying his life and Rebus is working his backside off. Cafferty rams this down Rebus's throat: he notes that he gives generously to charity and is happy, but Rebus – once retired – will be sitting in his flat with a scrap book of Cafferty cuttings.

While Rebus has his banter with Cafferty – and anyone else who comes down the pipe – the story continues. The discovery of the bodies at Fleshmarket Close is just another dark adventure from Edinburgh past; more important is the theme of racial tension. In fact it is the *vehemence* of the hatred within the racial tension that is important, and allows me to make a comparison to *Knots and Crosses*. Where I had criticised Rankin for underplaying the bad language of the SAS flashback scenes, I can't do the same for the racial tension scenes in *Fleshmarket Close*. They are powerful and full of tension and showcase the incredible journey as a writer Rankin had made throughout the Rebus series.

Rankin's success had allowed him to give up the day job and work full time on the novels. As the Rebus series came towards its conclusion – two books left to go at the time of *Fleshmarket Close* – Rankin told me that he had signed a two-book contract that would see him complete the series with one book a year. Yes, time was indeed running out for Detective Inspector John Rebus. Obscurity was just around the corner, while Rankin had progressed to having his own jacuzzi – although not purchased through ill-gotten gains – and living in a large, loving house.

Could Rebus change his predictable outcome? Perhaps not. Perhaps the old adage was true: a policeman's lot is not a happy one, and the poor Fifer who moved to Edinburgh for a better life retires lonely.

> 'By the way, Cafferty in *Fleshmarket Close* lives in my house… and last night I disturbed six intruders in the back garden. They were pissing about with Cafferty's jacuzzi – but not pissing in it, thank God!'
>
> *Author interview 5 November 2004*

CHAPTER TWENTY

THE G8 UNPLEASANTNESS

'I need to write a short story and a long essay before
I commence the next Rebus. It'll have G8 as its
backdrop, and that's about as much as I know.'

Author interview, 11 August 2005

As the books are set in real time, real events will inevitably be included to add to the reality, such as the 7/7 London bombings, the 2012 Olympic bid and George W. Bush falling off his bicycle whilst waving at police officers (Siobhan asking, 'Did we just do that?').

The title of *The Naming of the Dead* refers to the ceremony that Clarke's ageing left-wing parents attend, where a sampling of the names of the dead from the Iraq War is read out. But there are other lists too: the list of victims created by Rebus and Clarke as they try to unravel the crime and also to John Rebus' evocation of grief in naming the many of his own friends and family who have died in the course of his life (particularly his brother Michael, whose death overshadows the opening chapter).

So the 'naming of the dead' is a body count conveniently placed near the end of the series? No, nothing so bland, but it does provide a pause for thought on a much larger canvas: loss in its many guises – loss of love, friendship, youth, anger, hope. The facades of the characters melt away. They let their barriers down, so the reader can see who's really dead: those who fought in wars, in the Police Force, and our own families. For me personally, it is one of the very best novels in the Rebus series, because 'the naming of the dead' is there if you want it – and most of us do – but it is not rammed down one's throat. The writing is brilliantly understated. It normally is, but this one just hits all the right buttons for me. The main story is not hampered with over-sentimentality and Rebus is as off the wall as he always has been.

By the end of the book, Clarke realises that she has grown closer to understanding Rebus:

> "'It's not enough, is it?" she repeated. "Just…
> symbolic… because there's nothing else you can do."
> "What are you talking about?" he asked, with a smile.
> "The naming of the dead," she told him, resting her
> head against his shoulder.'

Siobhan increasingly fears that she is becoming more like him and consequently doomed to a similar fate:

> "'Obsessed and sidelined, thrawn and distrusted.
> Rebus had lost family and friends. When he went
> out drinking, he did so on his own, standing
> quietly at the bar, facing the row of optics."'

Siobhan knows her time with Rebus is coming to an end. And Rebus? Rebus is becoming more inward-looking, perhaps worrying a little more about his inevitable retirement. But no, no, Siobhan is not like Rebus. She wouldn't allow that to happen, but she may have picked up a few of his bad habits and how that will finally affect her future career remains to be seen.

Maybe the same people who wanted to hear more about Rebus after *Knots and Crosses* will want to hear more about Siobhan, but it's certainly to her that the future belongs, not to Rebus.

The book isn't just about the relationship between the characters: there's G8 too, along with other topics that were important to Rankin. 'How could I ignore the G8? It was the biggest thing to happen in my hometown in a generation; every cop in the city played a part. It was ready-made for Rebus to come stomping all over it. Besides, the books had been becoming more overtly political, and by using the G8 I could offer a few further observations.'

Like *Strip Jack*, *Let It Bleed, Black and Blue* and most of the others since *Resurrection Men, The Naming of the Dead* is a political novel.

How do the decisions made by the powers that be affect Scotland? Not just Edinburgh but the bigger picture? Where has Scottish industry gone? Where have the once vibrant mining towns gone? Indeed where have the busy shipyards, such as Rosyth, gone? Is it just 'progress' that has shut all this down? Was it just progress that wanted Scottish oil to fuel a war imposed by the British government? The one important point that *The Naming of the Dead* opens up for me is how little a voice Scotland has had in shaping its future over the past hundred years or so. It seems as though – and perhaps this is the optimism in Rankin's writing – that with G8 coming to Scotland, it was as if their collective voice was now beginning to be heard, that the Scottish Parliament suddenly had importance on the world stage.

'… First Minister of the Scottish Parliament was on the tarmac to greet the world leaders.'

The Naming of the Dead

CHAPTER TWENTY-ONE
EXIT WOUND

'The girl screamed once, only the once,
but it was enough.'

Exit Music

J ackie Leven's song 'John Rebus' depicts a lonely man by
its musical content alone – the kind of man we witnessed
sitting alone at the bar in *The Naming of the Dead*.

Most single men, when engrossed in a very busy –
intricate – working life, have no time to be lonely. They
have their occupation, colleagues and other distractions to
keep them busy. But what is interesting – with regards to
Rebus's self-contentment – is his thought processes at the
beginning of his last book, *Exit Music*. He meets with
another policeman who is due for retirement, not as
immediately as Rebus, but nevertheless *he* had major plans
for his retirement. He would become a taxi driver. Rebus is
quite clear that he wouldn't undertake such a profession,
but he thinks of the normal comforts of retirement – a

house, a wife, loving children nearby, or a complete escape to a foreign clime with a loved one – but none of that is applicable to him. He doesn't have his own home, he is divorced, and his child is living in sin in London while he is alone in Edinburgh.

Maybe Rebus could snatch some time with his friend Siobhan Clarke, but maybe she can get on with her own life and career now without him around.

So what is left? The pub?

A depressing picture begins to take shape and that is coupled with a sense of unfulfilment. Again, at the beginning of *Exit Music* there is Rebus making Clarke go through all his unfinished cases with him. Conversely, there is complete complacency, as Rebus and Clarke attend an autopsy and hardly take notice of what is going on. Rebus is tired. He is aware of the shortcomings in his life – personal and professional – but there is only so much that can be put right. In that respect he is a realist, but he has something of the cynic about him that keeps him away from pragmatism. So is he an underachiever? In a way, yes. He hasn't shaped his destiny the best way possible and he only has himself to blame for that.

Destiny is something Rebus blanks out as much as possible. His destiny has been shattered by his memories – those facts in his life that brought down his dreams. He was an underachiever in the SAS, an underachiever in relationships – from Rhona to anyone else he tries to court – and could have done better in the Police Force. There is a telling moment in *Death Is Not The End*, where he speculates that if he died that night he would leave nothing significant behind, and that made him want to drink: the last solace for the unhappy man.

So with that in mind, *Exit Music* is really about parting dignity – from the force, his colleagues and his enemies.

Enter 'Big Ger' Cafferty stage right. Rebus has had minor victories over Cafferty but a showdown between the two men was inevitable. It happened in *Exit Music* – to a degree – but that nagging feeling of unfinished business, underachievement – just a general feeling of discontent – is prevalent at the end for both the reader and John Rebus. And that in itself encapsulates Rebus's whole life, from our first meeting with him (where we learn about his premature exit from the SAS) to his ongoing, haphazard, disparate love life (peppered with booze, greasy food and too much hard work). Rebus is a stomach ulcer waiting to happen and he embodies many retiring police officers with bad habits and ruined relationships because of the intensity of the job. Although one could argue that he epitomises the retiring Scot, I would venture he epitomises the same type of creature in England, Wales and Ireland too. He is as much a victim of 'British' society as a self-wounding teenager with a low opinion of him/herself.

In 2007 I interviewed Leonard 'Nipper' Read, the arresting officer of the infamous Kray Twins and a man who also played his part in the capture of criminals working on The Great Train Robbery. Despite a high-profile career, Read told me that he was the victim of jealousy within the force that cost him a promised promotion, so even being a celebrity copper in the real world has its share of discontent.

And what about Siobhan?

I hate the cliché of unrequited love. Rebus is an older man, working with and influencing a much younger, not unattractive, intelligent woman. He will undoubtedly find her attractive or easy on the eye but he doesn't let that interfere with their relationship – personal or professional – and Siobhan respects him for that. My God, he *can* be a realist when he needs to be.

In a profession rife with sexism and one-upmanship, Rebus and Siobhan had found someone (each other) with the same moral code with regard to work, but completely different in age, gender and habits.

Some comparisons can be made between Siobhan and the young Gill Templer – and Gill had been his girlfriend – but all that strengthens is the argument that Rebus would find the lady attractive when younger. Let's be honest, if they had had a relationship, Siobhan would have probably gone the way of Gill: obtain her promotion and start pulling her hair out over John bloody Rebus!

> 'Goodyear was chatting to Siobhan Clarke now. Whatever he said made her laugh. Rebus decided it was time for a cigarette break and reached out to take Sonia's hand, planting a kiss on the back of it.'
>
> *Exit Music*

What is interesting is how Rebus and Siobhan's relationship will endure after Rebus leaves the force. In what way will they confide, socialise and interact with each other, and how will they cope with other people's opinion of that relationship? There is a bond between them that the intensity of their work has forged. Their lives have been in each other's hands and, perhaps, that is the mutual understanding as to how they will take their own lives forward. And there lies the rub: Siobhan and Rebus house the perfect platonic relationship. And one thing is for certain, she will shed a tear when he dies, because she knows that he really loved her but never admitted it.

Do we get any of this information from *Exit Music* itself? Yes. That one moment before Rebus takes Sonia's hand. It's left unsaid but it's symbolic because spiritually, Rebus has just let go of Siobhan's hand.

> '... he couldn't see himself ever leaving
> Edinburgh. It was the oxygen in his bloodstream,
> but still with mysteries to be explored.'
>
> *Exit Music*

Exit Music is set in the late autumn of Edinburgh and the career of DI John Rebus. We find him trying to tie up the loose ends of his career but being thwarted by the murder of a Russian poet. Even though Rebus's career is coming to an end, the crimes on the streets of Edinburgh continue – a humbling notion surely, as he must have originally set out, like most young cops, to bring crime to a grinding stop!

A key aspect of the novel is a Russian delegation coming to Edinburgh in order to bring new business to the city, an interesting point when one considers a Russian has just been killed in Edinburgh. Somebody doesn't want progress...

So much has changed in Scotland since Rebus joined the force but there is one constant: 'Big Ger' Cafferty. It has been Cafferty's presence that has kept Rebus's spark of duty alive, almost as if the gangster's presence keeps Rebus somehow in line. He would never jeopardise his career if he knew that there was a genuine possibility of putting Cafferty behind bars once and for all.

There is a synergy between the cop and the gangster and the nuances of this are not appreciated until Cafferty is beaten up with only days to go before Rebus retirement. Surely he is to blame? Even the good guys think that he was behind it. And doesn't this hark back to the first Rebus novel, where we believe Rebus could be the murderer?

Cafferty dies at the hospital but Rebus is there and he fights to bring his nemesis back because he needs a big showdown – he wants blood and pain, not a death in sleep. Death in sleep was for Rebus to endure at the end of retirement, not 'Big Ger'!

Rebus hangs on to Cafferty's life because it is one of the few things left that make sense in his own life. He remembers how he got the name Strawman: when called to the dock to give evidence against Cafferty, somebody called the wrong name – which sounded like Strawman – and Cafferty had called him that ever since. And as the lyrics of Lou Reed's song would dictate, a Strawman would go straight to the Devil and then straight on to hell. 'I'll see you there, Strawman, third piece of fiery brimstone to the left. Just me and you, slugging it out for eternity.'

IAN RANKIN AND INSPECTOR REBUS

The interesting thing about *Exit Music* is that as Rebus spirals to his doomsday, Siobhan Clarke gets immersed deeper into the thought processes that would make her a much better police officer – she has a future, Rebus doesn't. But she has something of Rebus's unorthodox approach to her; something has indeed rubbed off from the sorcerer to the apprentice, which in a way proves that the system doesn't really work. Rules have to be broken occasionally.

Siobhan didn't start out a cynic or a maverick and, although time will tell if these influences will prevail, she can at least see them and understand them. She will have to choose what course she wants to follow in the future. By being with Rebus, she has grown up very quickly, gained much experience – was it too much too soon? No, of course it wasn't, but that trait of cynicism would be with her for a little while yet… won't it, John?

The quote from *Exit Music* at the head of this chapter brings the Rebus series full circle. It is the opening line of the novel and echoes the opening line of the very first Rebus novel *Knots and Crosses*: 'The girl screamed once, only once.'

One can always over-analyse the change of writing style, speculating that if Rankin rewrote *Knots and Crosses*, he would lengthen the original opening line to give more rhythm and allow the reader to dwell on the verb. Frankly, he probably changed it deliberately on nothing more than a whim. But the following story would show less cut and thrust and more subtlety within the sub-text. Rankin has commented on – analysed – his own novels (see *Rebus's Scotland* at least), and through writing about Rebus for 20 years and at least as many novels, novellas and other collections, he would know more – and ostensibly have more to say – about the character and his profession. In short, we are talking confidence here. Rankin is so familiar with his characters, at ease with his own style – gently explaining the odd Scottish word or phrase – that there is a natural flow that comes from all Rebus novels. From *Black and Blue* onwards? No, from the very beginning, but as far as my personal enjoyment is concerned, from *The Black Book* onwards – the book that introduced St Leonard's,'Big Ger' and Siobhan Clarke.

Finally, is *Exit Music* a grand finale for John Rebus, or is it an anti-climax? That's an interesting question and one I posed to Rankin.

'The version of *Exit Music* I handed to my editor ended with Rebus at the railway station. My editor begged me to take Rebus back to the hospital for one last scene with "Big Ger". I think that worked. Maybe it's better than the original ending; maybe it's just a different ending.'

But can Rankin let Rebus go?

'It's funny but with *The Complaints* [the next big novel after *Exit Music*], the story takes place in the Edinburgh police HQ... and I can sort of feel Rebus's presence just through the walls; maybe in the next office or corridor along, or one flight up; or in the canteen. He's still working somewhere, he hasn't left the building.'

But is this indeed The End for Rebus, as there is a new character that populates Rankin's novels?

'Let's see what the future brings,' Rankin says. 'My new character is an Internal Affairs cop. There are a few skeletons in Rebus's closet, aren't there? Who knows, maybe Internal Affairs will come knocking on his door one fine day... [lxxi]

> 'I never forget a face, but in your case I'll be glad to make an exception.'
>
> *Groucho Marx*

---

lxxi Author interview 26 July 2009.

CHAPTER TWENTY-TWO

YOU CAN'T ALWAYS GET WHAT YOU WANT

"'You've known Cafferty a long time," Stone said.
"Nigh on twenty years."
"You first gave evidence against him in Glasgow
High Court."
"That's right. Bloody lawyer got me mixed up with the
previous witness, called me 'Mr Stroman.' After that,
Cafferty's nickname for me was Strawman."
"Like in The Wizard of Oz?'"

Exit Music

'You asked me right at the beginning of this interview: how many more books are left? Well, the time to finish the series realistically is when I haven't got anything new to find out about Rebus, when he's got nothing new to show me, or he becomes tedious to write about and I've got nothing new to say about Edinburgh through his eyes.'

Rankin told me this during my *Fleshmarket Close* interview. At the time I thought he was cranking himself up for a Rebus in retirement set of books but he kept assuring me that he didn't know — never knew in fact — what the next book was going to be about until he started it. In

August 2009, shortly after the proofs of *The Complaints* had gone off and the hardback was awaiting release, he told me that he still didn't know what the next book would be. He was determined to have a year off: he wasn't going to write another graphic novel (because he didn't enjoy the experience much), he still didn't know if he was going to continue with Siobhan, but the new character – Inspector Malcolm Fox – intrigued him and as Rankin told me in July 2009, there were enough skeletons in Rebus's closet to warrant investigation...

In truth, there were probably too many avenues open to Rankin. He wanted to do a funny 18th-century Edinburgh novel (an extension of a radio play he had written). He had told me – or rather teased me – that he could dust off *Summer Rites* and make it fit for publication (his wife did think it one of his best novels)! He could even find the original manuscript of *Westwind* – so radically different from the published version – and release that for the first time (although that didn't cross his mind, it crossed mine!). Again, so many options. A real literary mid-life crisis, i.e. did he want to tie himself down for another 20 years with a new character? Or did he want to go back over old ground and continue Rebus through a series about Siobhan?

The subject was so broad we had to discuss it:

So why don't you kill Rebus off and be done with it?
'I had an irate woman come up to me at a signing in Edinburgh and she said, "Don't you dare get rid of Rebus! Don't you dare! I don't like that Siobhan, so don't you dare," and for some people the characters are very real to

them. It's almost like they'd be losing a friend if he died. In fact the characters are probably more real to them than I am to them!'

Didn't Conan Doyle have this problem? In fact he killed off Sherlock Holmes!
'He did indeed. He killed him off at the Reichenbach Falls and had to bring him back because the fans demanded it. So perhaps I'll put Rebus over the Reichenbach Falls!'

I dare you! Yes but he killed him off and then wrote The Hound of the Baskervilles.
'Yeah, good move wasn't it? Commercially it was good, but was it good for his soul?'

(It may be a bit of literary banter but Rankin nearly gave Rebus a Reichenbach ending towards the end of *Strip Jack*. There is a scene where Rebus is running through a forest in the dead of night when suddenly the moon breaks through clouds and he notices that he is about to plummet off a plateau into a river. Then suddenly the murderer comes out of nowhere, hurtling towards him... well, there was the opportunity!)

OK, you're taking the piss now!
'I honestly don't know what is going to happen next. When I had five books to go before Rebus retired, I didn't know if I was going to kill him off in the very next one!'

In August 2003 Rankin told me that if Rebus retired when

Rankin was 48, then he would have plenty of time to write other things that interested him. It was then that he told me about his historical novel.

'I've got plenty of time to write comedies, historical novels – I would love to write about 18th-century Edinburgh – it was a fascinating time, lots of men of genius running around, and people escaping the guillotine in France running around. A real hotchpotch – there was a judge who kept a pig as a pet, Sir Walter Scott running around, just mad, mad times in Edinburgh and that would be interesting to do as a comedy. I've done something similar for radio with a private eye and it was good fun.'

Rankin could write an historical novel next. He is after all a frustrated historian anyway: books such as *Strip Jack* have characters by the name of Knox (as in John Knox) and his Rebus series started with homages to Robert Louis Stevenson, as did his new series. *The Complaints* brings Stevenson's classic *Kidnapped* to mind with character names such as Breck and Fox (Red Fox) and a location of Queensferry (OK, Rankin uses Queensferry a lot but the comparison is there if you want it) and Heriot Row is suggested very early on too.

So what is certain?
'I'll keep writing. It's how I make sense of the world. People think you're in it for the money, but there gets to a stage where you've got all the money you need. J K Rowling, she'll keep writing and it's not just audience pressure – it's almost like a therapy. You're giving shape to chaos, the chaos around you.'

CONCLUSION
LET IT BLEED

'I do not write for the public; I do write for money, a
noble deity; and most of all for myself, not perhaps any
more noble but both more intelligent and nearer home.
Let us tell each other sad stories of the bestiality of
the beast whom we feed... there must be something
wrong in me, or I would not be popular.'

Robert Louis Stevenson, January 1886

Like most writers, Ian Rankin tantalises and teases his
audience with little snippets of his own life within his
famous character John Rebus, but Rebus isn't Rankin.
The author had no flirtation with National Service,
although family and childhood friends would. He didn't
join the Police Force, although his imagination very early
on took him into the insalubrious world of crime and
social comment.

Rankin says that he sympathises with the character
Siobhan Clarke more than Rebus, stating that he was
closer in age to that character so therefore had more in
common. I think there is more to it than that. What I see

in Rankin – in his impressionable High School and university years – is a respect for the older, wiser man. As Conan Doyle looked up to his Sherlock Holmes, Rankin looked up to his Rebus. But Rebus was not one person as Dr Joseph Bell was the single prototype for Holmes. He was a pastiche, no, a puzzle – a rebus – made up, not of pictures of symbols, but of several English teachers and authors he knew in his formative years, perhaps those mentioned at the beginning of this book, who guided and shaped his literary talents. As Siobhan Clarke is tutored in her profession by Rebus, Rankin was tutored in his trade by his mentors.

> "'Justice never sleeps, Siobhan. Which doesn't mean
> you shouldn't. Anything I can get you before I go?"
> "A sense of having achieved something, maybe?'"

In the above quote from *A Question of Blood*, Siobhan is in hospital, not Rebus, but although she has made sacrifices and ended up hurt, she still needs the reassurances of her mentor. So does Rankin need those reassurances too? Not in a physical sense, no. But he has adopted Edinburgh as his hometown nowadays and that comes with baggage: the statues, homes and myths of novelists past are the altar he preaches at. The history, mixed with the crime, intrigue and legend of Scotland's capital city, is what thrills Rankin. He analyses the legends of Deacon Brodie, Burke and Hare – all true-life villains – and then wallows in the literary legends of yesteryear too. He will speak of Spark, Welsh, Stevenson, Scott, Hogg, Conan Doyle and Burns in his interviews, as he told me, 'because I have a fascination for books. I was just fascinated by them, and writing.'[lxxii]

It's all good stuff but if that is the final conclusion to this book, then I think we're missing the magic. Let us dig a little deeper into the light of our findings.

Rebus is an exploration into Rankin's alternative careers. The author is simply exorcising the ghosts of his subconscious close escape. Too deep? Let's rationalise: the young lad from Cardenden who felt different, didn't want the natural career path of the Armed Forces or Police Force, so he became the first person in his family ever to go to university. Not only did he go there, he did well and worked hard on his fiction to make it his livelihood, and as his fame became greater, so did his desire to write about Rebus and exorcise any semblance of those beckoning careers. But then he begins to distance himself from Rebus, making him deliberately different from him.

To take it further, Rebus is the older, dissatisfied Rankin from a parallel world, the man who didn't escape.

Rebus will only see a never-ceasing wave of crime extending beyond his retirement. He comes to realise by *Exit Music* that he wasn't as important to the system as he initially felt. All those self-sacrifices to his personal life meant little. New Detective Inspectors are made and he is destined to go the way of all flesh once retired: as insignificant but as beautifully tragic as any other human being throughout history. Everybody has their flaws – even

---

lxxii Author interview March 2001.

Bono – and everyone has to finally call it a day and let the young (and sometimes innovative) take over.

Rebus has kept Rankin focused on what has gone right in his life. Unlike Rebus, Rankin is still married, close to his children, thankful for his success, and shares his stories and perceptions with fans and journalists alike, sometimes over a beer or coffee.

'I suppose I'm a bit like Rebus,' Rankin explained, 'but not as street smart. However, I would have made a lousy cop – I get too involved in things, so the nature of the work would get to me.'[lxxiii]

Rankin appears egoless, but he cherishes his status and home life, because those are the true ingredients that success is based upon. His constant analysis of Edinburgh is as cynical as Stevenson's *Edinburgh: Picturesque Notes*. Like Stevenson, Rankin moved south to England and then overseas, but unlike Stevenson, Rankin returned. Perhaps he saw more worth in his home country than his predecessor, or perhaps it's just a sign of the times – the restless spirit returns home.

The growth of the welfare state has taken people out of the gutter but crime – grime – homelessness and violence are still endemic everywhere and Scotland is no exception. Rankin has almost seen it as his quest to break through the veneer of the picturesque tartan tin to expose this underbelly, which lives and breathes outside the small protective bubble of tourist Edinburgh. The Rebus series took the sting out of *Trainspotting* but not the cynicism.

---

lxxiii Author interview March 2002.

Many things are changing in Scotland and Rankin is at the forefront of the literary change inspired by the cultural changes. He has a right to be xenophobic, or at least be deeply wrapped up and proud of his adopted city, because he has an important job to do: to raise the literary profile of the country and by doing so, expose and tackle its many social issues.

Scotland isn't just a location for one's holidays. It's a place with good and bad history (like everywhere else), with people funny and sad, good and bad, and above all, hearts and souls with important things to say.

Maybe, if the many branches of Waterstones in London had a section dedicated to Scottish literature, then part of Rankin's inner quest would be fulfilled. I say this because he – quite rightly in my opinion – always searches to justify every aspect of Scottish literature, but it's got to be modern literature, not just the classics. *Trainspotting* should sit next to *Heart of Midlothian*, *The Wasp Factory* with *The Confessions of a Justified Sinner*, *Strange Case of Dr Jekyll and Mr Hyde* with *Knots and Crosses*, *All That Really Matters* with *Burns Poetry*, and *The Prime of Miss Jean Brodie* with *The Hound of the Baskervilles*. And so it goes on…

Ian Rankin acknowledges the Scots' denial of all things good or bad in their lives because his worldwide fame dictates that he must (any denial on Rankin's part would be churlish to say the least). And that's another important point: Rebus is the underbelly of Rankin, the cynic that keeps him so well balanced.

'Rebus knew his own criteria came cheaply: his flat, books, music and clapped-out car. And he realised that he had reduced his life to a mere shell in recognition that he had completely failed at the important things: love, relationships, family life.'

The Hanging Garden

And it is the latter things in the above quote that Rankin has made a success of.

So finally, what part of the 20 Rebus books do we conclude makes Ian Rankin John Rebus? None. He was just an exploration. An unplanned bit of this and bit of that. The answer is in the name: Rebus. A picture puzzle but still only a snap shot. Rebus drank a little too much and Rankin did himself for a while – no crime or revelation there. They both love rock music – namely The Rolling Stones – and perhaps just like their rock 'n' roll heroes, they can't get no satisfaction.

So what *is* my final conclusion? Simply that Rebus is a character we've all had a lot of fun with – including his creator – and has allowed us all to look at the real Edinburgh, the city that lies beneath the veneer. Rebus has been our tour guide on a Beatles-like magical mystery tour and, along with his creator Ian Rankin, we've all enjoyed the ride. But once Rankin knew he had fulfilled his dream of becoming an international bestselling writer, he moved away from identifying with Rebus, or giving him some of the same memories as his creator, and that was because Ian Rankin was a different man. He wasn't

THE BIRTH OF
JOHN REBUS

During March 2001 I interviewed Ian Rankin to promote his novel *The Falls*. During this interview he spoke very openly about his childhood ambition to become a writer and how he dismissed the Armed Forces and Police Force as a career, which was the usual career path for a lad from Cardenden. Rankin was certainly on form during this interview, as he explained to me how Rebus came out of this mix as his alter ego!

Although I have covered the main points Rankin made to me during that interview in the text of this book, there is a validity in transcribing this segment of the interview tape so fans can hear it straight from the author himself. When I went back over the tape in my research for this book, I was pleased to find that the angle I had chosen had been, in a way, predicted by our interview seven years previous and, therefore, as an Annex, this interview reinforces the suppositions I have made and also lets Rankin have the last say on the matter.

Slainte!

The Rebus books are as much about Edinburgh as they are about Rebus — would you agree?
'Absolutely. I went to Edinburgh aged 18 to go to university. I was born and brought up in a coal-mining town 30 miles north of Edinburgh. I went there as a student and I was living on the outskirts in this quite rough area, because Edinburgh is ringed by these places. But the centre of town isn't allowed to change. Tourists go there and they see Greyfriars Bobby, the Scott Monument, the castle; then hear some bagpipe music, buy some shortbread and go home, right? And in the late '70s, early '80s, there was this other Edinburgh where some of the housing estates were so bad Oxfam were running aid convoys in. No joke. It had the worst Aids, HIV and heroin injection problem in Western Europe per capita. A huge problem. And nobody was writing about it, nobody was talking about it. The Edinburgh people were talking about was the Edinburgh of Miss Jean Brodie, and Jekyll and Hyde and Walter Scott, so I wanted to tackle the unseen Edinburgh.

Where did the idea come from that Rebus should have been a veteran of the Armed Forces?
'I have always been fascinated by the Armed Forces. My

family for example: my two sisters married into the RAF. One husband was in the RAF from the age of 15 to 50 and served all over the globe and I used to get great holidays as a consequence. I went to places such as Cyprus and Malta, and I'd always been fascinated by it. When I was ten years old I wrote away for all the Army career information, and I got all the packs and career stuff back.

'The area I lived in in Fife was quite rough, and when I left school a lot of the guys joined the Police Force or the Armed Forces, because they were the only opportunities open to them. Rosyth naval dockyard was nearby, so it did make sense. And in that way Rebus was a bit of an alter ego: he was a bit like me if I hadn't gone to university, [the] things I might have done with myself if I hadn't taken that leap – because I was the first person in my family to go to university. I might well have joined the police, or the Army or the RAF. Actually I wouldn't have joined the RAF, I'm scared of heights!'

But why did you go to university?
'I had a fascination for books. I was just fascinated by them, and writing. From the age of four or five I was trying to write comic books, song lyrics later on for a band that didn't exist, except inside my head. So I did English at uni because it meant I could just sit around and read books and get paid for it! I had a student grant to sit around all day and read the books I would have sat around and read anyway. So I was quite fixed from an early age really, as far as what I wanted to be. I had seen my sister and the life she had married into in the Armed Forces. She was a year or two

here and a year or two there and they never owned their own home. It was always Armed Forces commissions and carpets and everybody on the camp had the same house. And I saw all of this as a kid and I thought, I don't want that. I want stability. For the kind of writer I wanted to be, I wanted stability in my life.

'They [my sister and her husband] have had a great life. They've travelled the world and now both of their sons have gone into the RAF, so both of my nephews have followed that path. And so, with Rebus, I wanted to give him an interesting background, and I wanted to make him older than me. I was 22 or 23; he was going to be in his forties. In the first book he is 40. And he'd been married and all that kind of stuff, and I just wanted to give him a past, and there came the Jekyll and Hyde thing. There was this Hyde character that was really close to him but who eventually grows to hate him and tries to kill him. And the book was very consciously based upon Jekyll and Hyde to that extent, so I thought if he'd been through the Army training and the SAS training – and I had been reading books about the SAS – then part of it was the psychological warfare, where they try to break you and that can be fairly traumatic. I thought that that would be a great way to have this guy crack up [the Hyde character] and so they went from being brothers-in-arms to having some great divide between them. Hyde believes that he was sold out by Rebus and comes to hate him.

'So it all just clicked together like that and meant that he wasn't just a dyed-in-the wool cop. He [Rebus] went through the SAS Parachute Regiment, cracked up under it, had a breakdown and decided to join the police – or was pushed into joining the police to keep him out of trouble – but he wasn't part of the police machinery, so it was a nice way of making him an outsider as well, but making sure that he was fit enough and tough enough to take on the modern-day drug dealer and gangster.

'I still have no idea what he looks like!'

REBUS ON SCREEN

Rebus was the title of the detective drama based on the Inspector Rebus novels and was produced by STV Productions (previously known as SMG Productions) for the ITV Network. The show lasted just shy of eight years, spread over four series, being cancelled in February 2008 after Ken Stott announced that he didn't want to play the part any more.

The first series starred John Hannah and was made for STV by his own production company, Clerkenwell Films. A new cast featuring Ken Stott as DI Rebus was introduced in the second series (which went into production in 2005 and was made in-house by STV).

For me, and although each episode of the show was nicely made with quality actors, the storylines were pale counterparts to Rankin's novels. Clearly you can't put into a TV show the fine detail of a novel, but in the case of *Rebus* there was a distinct lack of depth to certain stories. In this Annex you will find the basic production history of the show preceded by a short observation regarding each episode, not necessarily a review of the action, which has little regard for Rankin's original novels. All of this serves as a basic reference for anyone wanting to know more about the show.[lxxiv]

The show is not without its critics, especially episodes such as *Fleshmarket Close, The Hanging Garden* and *The Falls*, where the stories seemed rushed and lacked any tension. The fact that two actors played Rebus in such a short time implies that the series' makers never really found the right formula for the show. The fact that there is little description of Rebus in the novels gives the reader the freedom to picture the Inspector any way they wish, which probably means that whoever plays him on screen won't come up to every fan's individual expectation.

Many fans of the books got confused or disillusioned by the series. Due to this lack of enthusiasm for the show, I open this Annex with a short interview with Rankin about his perception of the TV series.

---

lxxiv The cast and crew lists printed in Annex are taken directly from the beginning and end credits of the TV show and some inconsistencies were noted regarding spelling of surnames. I have attempted to rationalise this to provide a uniform approach throughout.

RANKIN ON *REBUS*

What do you think of the TV series?

'Well, they pulled my anti-terrorist story from the screen because of 9/11, which is strange because I thought that was one of the more old-fashioned stories in the series (*Mortal Causes*), in as much as things have changed so much in Northern Ireland. The situations have changed, the gangs have changed and the book was written and set in the 1990s, even though they changed it quite a bit for TV! I had a walk-on part in it and it was eventually shown in 2004.'

What was your part?

'I walked past John Hannah (Rebus) in the street! Of the first three stories of the original series, I watched the first one *Black and Blue* at the time and liked it, but I didn't watch the other three.'

Why was that?

'I think I was worried that if I let the TV series get too much under my skin it would change the way I wrote the books.

'Before the stuff went on TV I spoke to a few crime writers who had been on the box [TV] and the general consensus was to try and stay away from it. Keep away from the filming of it, don't get too involved, because of necessity TV will change your characters to fit its own parameters. And they end up not being your characters.'

But the books are radically different from the TV series?

'A lot of the Rebus books take place inside Rebus's head and I didn't want to start hearing an actor's voice and seeing an actor in front of me and that worried me a lot. John Hannah [the first screen Rebus] was so different from my idea of Rebus in terms of age; it wasn't a big problem for me in that respect. My Rebus was 55 at the time of the first series and John Hannah was 39. So it was kind of watching a young Rebus, not the person I was writing about.'

As long as you can still detach yourself from the series in that way, it is OK?
'Yes, but some writers can't. There was a terrible case where the writer of the Anna Lee mysteries – Liza Cody – found the screen character far too pretty. And because the actress was nothing like the character, Liza couldn't write about her any more. She let her go and invented somebody else.'

So on that basis you were always a bit shy of watching the Rebus shows?
'Yes, just a wee bit. I certainly didn't want anyone to change my ideas, and I always imagined a TV series as living in a parallel universe anyway. It's another interpretation. Everyone has another interpretation of what Rebus was like, and the TV series was exactly that.'

So it's really the luck of the draw, as far as TV is concerned, if you're going to get a good interpretation or a bad one?
'The Rebus books were first picked up by the BBC. They were the first to cast it and I went down to London from Edinburgh to see the big cheeses for a casting meeting, and they asked me who I thought should play Rebus. I told them that I had absolutely no idea what he looked like. However,

his background was SAS and he was a bit tough and they said that they were thinking of Robbie Coltrane. And I smiled a bit, thinking that the flashbacks to Rebus's SAS training would be brilliant – the assault course with Private Robbie Coltrane running over it!'

SERIES 1

Black and Blue 26 April 2000
The Hanging Garden 6 September 2000
Dead Souls 13 September 2001
Mortal Causes 1 November 2004 (this episode was postponed from 20 September 2001 due to the 9/11 attacks on the US in 2001).

Main characters

Detective Inspector John Rebus: John Hannah
Detective Sergeant Siobhan Clarke: Gayanne Potter
Detective Chief Inspector Gill Templer: Sara Stewart
Detective Inspector Jack Morton: Ewan Stewart
Morris Gerald Cafferty: James Cosmo

SERIES 2

The Falls 2 January 2006
Fleshmarket Close 6 March 2006

SERIES 3

The Black Book 8 September 2006
A Question of Blood 15 September 2006
Strip Jack 22 September 2006
Let it Bleed 29 September 2006

SERIES 4

Resurrection Men 5 October 2007
The First Stone 12 October 2007
The Naming of the Dead 26 October 2007
Knots and Crosses 7 December 2007

Main characters

Detective Inspector John Rebus: Ken Stott
Detective Chief Inspector Gill Templer: Jennifer Black
Detective Sergeant Siobhan Clarke: Claire Price

PLOT SUMMARIES

Black and Blue

The story starts with a man being tied to a chair by two thugs, tools being taken from a bag and the victim escaping by throwing himself out of the window while still tied to the chair. He plunges several floors.

Rebus has labelled a serial killer as a 'copycat' of '60s murderer Bible John. He gathers his leads in the case while drinking heavily and overcoming his inner demons. Sitting in his living room, looking through his netless window at the Edinburgh night sky, there is a feeling as if the city is willing him to drink himself to an early grave, but the telephone rings as if the living are telling him that he's still needed.

The scenes of darkness, rain and disquiet make this an entertaining, atmospheric and pacy episode, albeit a shadow of its original story.

A fictionalised version of The Dancing Pigs – the punk band Rankin sang for – appears briefly in this episode. The title refers to the Rolling Stones album *Black and*

Blue, which is briefly seen in the story. Over all, an entertaining show.

CAST

DI John Rebus John Hannah, *Ryan Slocum (The Preacher)* Jim Norton, *DI Morton* Ewan Stewart, *DCI Templer* Sara Stewart, *Eve Kendall* Joanna Roth, *D Supt McCaskill* Stuart Hepburn, *DS Clarke* Gayanne Potter, *Angie Riddell* Clare McCaron, *Lawson Geddes* David Lyon, *Lenny Spaven* Robert McIntosh, *DI Ormond* Lewis Howden, *Barry Judd* Fish, *Joanne McKenzie* Jenny Foulds, *Paul Martin (The Disciple)* Stevie Hannon, *D Supt Grogan* David Gallacher, *DI Lumsden* Gilbert Martin, *WPC Logan* Jenny Ryan, *Stanley Toal* Stephen McCole, *Joe Toal* Michael Carter, *Alan Mitchison* Russell Anderson, *Mark Jenkins* Graeme Mearns, *Tony Kane* Andrew McCulloch, *Mental Minto* Anthony Donaldson, *Kenny Lynch* Malcolm Shields, *Rico Briggs* Tam White, *William 'Craw' Crawford* Billy Barclay, *DC McLean* Andrew John Tait, *TV Presenter* Nicola Burnett Smith, *Taxi Driver* Richard Callum, *Hotel Owner* Alistair Ritchie, *Customs Officer* Paul Pirie, *Gerry the Waiter* John Leith, *Undertaker* Colin Scott-Moncrieff, *Ronnie Singh* Faroque Khan, *Venessa* Molly Innes, *TV Journalist* Ian Sexon, *Immigration Officer* Ian Cairns.

Standby Props Chris McMillan and Tristan Carlisle-Kitz, *Props Driver* Andy Neilson, *Dressing Props* Bobb Orr and John Casey, *Prop Master* Bill Gower, *Standby Carpenter* Ian Gallacher, *Standby Painter* John Hughes, *Standby Rigger* John Rhymer, *Construction Painter* Henry Gallacher, *Construction Manager* Malcolm Gilbert, *Electricians* Joe McLean, Ben Horsefield, *Genny Operator* Phil Green, *Best*

IAN RANKIN AND INSPECTOR REBUS

Boy Eddie Monaghan, *Lighting Gaffer* Bob Horsefield, *Floor Runner* Emmet Cahill, *Third Assistant Director* Mark Murdoch, *Second Assistant Director* Dee Hellier, *Script Supervisor* Sheila Johnston, *Production Runner* Mark McGhee, *Production Secretary* Claire Gammon, *Production Co-ordinator* Joanne O'Sullivan, *Assistant Accountant* Lorraine Berrie, *Production Accountant* Wim De Greff, *Location Runner* Robert Cowie, *Unit Manager* Miglet Crichton, *Location Manager* Brian Kaczynski, *Assistant Film Editor* Laura Gorman, *Dubbing Mixer* Chris Sinclair, *Sound Editor* Douglas MacDougall, *Graphic Design* Douglas Bryce, *Post Production Supervisor* Liz Pearson, *Stunts* David Andres and Vincent Keane, *Stunt Co-ordinator* Roderick P Woodruff, *Special Effects Designer* Paul Kelly for Any Effects, *Special Effects Supervisor* Tom Harris, *Wardrobe Assistant* Nicholas Roache-Gordon, *Costume Supervisor* Suzy Freeman, *Boom Operator* Bradley Kendrick, *Sound Recordist* Brian Milliken, *2nd Camera Assistant* Joe Blackwell, *2nd Camera Operator* Dave Carey, *Grip* Terry Pate, *Clapper Loader* Stephen Warner, *Focus Puller* Steve Oxley, *First Assistant Director* Nael Abbas, *Casting Director* Di Carling CDG, *Screenplay* Stuart Hepburn, *Script Editor* Nicole Cauverien, *Costume Designer* Delphine Roche-Gordon, *Make-Up Designer* Amanda Warburton and Alison Davies, *Music* Douglas Ferguson, *Editor* Chris Buckland, *Director of Photography* Doug Hallows, *Production Designer* Campbell Gordon, *Line Producer* Gary Tuck, *Director* Martyn Friend, *Producer* Murray Ferguson, *Executive Producer* Philip Hinchcliffe and John Hannah.

The Hanging Garden

The film has a violent but very atmospheric opening that sensitively bastardises the important points at the start of the novel.

The voice-over from Hannah is good and helps gel a highly charged story. 'Big Ger' is OK, Tommy Telford, more so. A lot of Rebus's complex love life is left unsaid to keep the story visual and at pace. From the mid-point of the film the pace is somewhat increased and more detail is left out, including a character full of Eastern promise…

Overall *The Hanging Garden* is a very watchable TV drama, even if Templer's character is taken far from the original books, but then again some liberties were taken with some of the nicely tied loose ends at the end of the original novel.

Note: the book title refers to The Cure's song 'The Hanging Garden'.

CAST

DI John Rebus John Hannah, *DI Morton* Ewan Stewart, *DCI Templer* Sara Stewart, *DI Ormond* Lewis Howden, *D Supt McCaskill* Stuart Hepburn, *DS Clarke* Gayanne Potter, *Dr Emir Slaven* Tom Watson, *Candice/Katarina* Sheyla Shehovich, *Morris Cafferty* James Cosmo, *Sammy Rebus* Eilidh MacDonald, *DI Miriam Kenworthy* Philippa Watson, *Jake Tarawicz* Deka Walmsley, *Tommy Telford* Tommy Flanagan, *'Pretty Boy' Summers* Scott Cleverdon, *Rhona* Corinne Harris, *WPC Logan* Jenny Ryan, *Executive* Jaclyn Tse, *Weasel* Andrew Barr, *Kenny Houston* Douglas Russell, *Sean Haddow* James G O'Hara, *Telford Man* Martyn Tim Webster, *Danny Simpson*

Steve Caswell, *DS Bill Pryde* Robert Paterson, *Doctor* Jacques Kerr, *Nurse* Trish Mullin, *Boy Eyewitness* Sean Mowat, *Acid Throwing Man* Chris Young, *Marty* Rab Affleck, *Taxi Driver* Gordon Munro, *Singer* Owen Gorman, *A&E Doctor* Patrick Logan, *Boy* Scott Weir.

Standby Props Chris McMillan and Dennis Knotts, *Props Driver* Andy Neilson, *Dressing Props* Bob Orr and John Brown, *Prop Master* Bill Gower, *Standby Carpenter* Ian Gallacher, *Standby Painter* John Hughes, *Standby Rigger* Peter Callaghan, *Construction Painter* Henry Gallagher, *Construction Manager* Malcolm Gilbert, *Art Department Runner* Sarah Cowlishaw, *Production Buyer* Douglas Harvey, *Art Directors* Nicki McCallum and Catherine Carruthers, *Electricians* Joe McLean and Mike Archer, *Genny Operator* Phil Green, *Best Boy* Eddie Monaghan, *Lighting Gaffer* Bob Horsefield, *Floor Runner* Emmet Cahill, *Third Assistant Director* Mark Murdoch, *Second Assistant Director* Dee Hellier, *Script Supervisor* Sheila Johnston, *Production Runner* Mark McGhee, *Production Secretary* Claire Gammon, *Production Co-ordinator* Joanne O'Sullivan, *Assistant Accountant* Lorraine Berrie, *Production Accountant* Wim De Greef, *Location Runner* Robert Cowie, *Unit Manager* Miglet Crichton, *Location Manager* Brian Kaczynski, *Assistant Film Editor* Laura Gorman, *Dubbing Mixer* Chris Sinclair, *Sound Editor* Douglas MacDoughall, *Post Production Supervisor* Liz Pearson, *Stunts* David Anders, Theo Kypri, Lex Milloy, Andy J Smart, Trevor Steedman, Tony van Silva and Len Woodcock, *Stunt Co-ordinator* Roderick P Woodruff, *Special Effects Designer* Paul Kelly for Any Effects, *Special Effects Supervisor* Tom Harris, *Armourer* Gregg Pearson, *Armourers* Perdix Firearms, *Wardrobe Assistant* Nicholas Roche-Gordon, *Costume*

Supervisor Suzy Freedman, *Boom Operator* Bradley Kendrick, *Sound Recordist* Brian Milliken, *2nd Camera Assistant* Joe Blackwell, *Steadicam/2nd Camera Operator* Dave Carey, *Clapper Operator* Stephen Warner, *Focus Puller* Steve Oxley, *Grip* Terry Pate, *First Assistant Director* Nael Abbas, *Casting Director* Di Carling CDG, *Screenplay* Ben Brown and Philip Palmer, *Script Editor* Nicole Cauverien, *Costume Designer* Delphine Roche-Gordon, *Make-up Designer* Alison Davies and Amanda Warburton, *Music* David Ferguson, *Editor* Chris Buckland, *Director of Photography* Doug Hallows, *Production Designer* Campbell Gordon, *Director* Maurice Phillips, *Line Producer* Gary Tuck, *Producer* Murray Ferguson, *Executive Producers* Philip Hinchcliffe and John Hannah.

Dead Souls

Rebus's troubled sleep — dark and gothic — opens the story. But soon Rebus springs into action and starts to narrate the story.

He arrests a known paedophile, Darren Rough, as he takes photographs at the zoo. Rebus thinks he is taking photos of children but in fact he is taking photos of the animals. Rebus and DI Jim Margolies take Darren home, arousing the local community as to his past at the same time — so much so that Darren eventually needs police protection.

Old school friend Barny Mee turns up at St Leonard's to ask Rebus for help in locating his missing son. Rebus is reluctant to help until he finds that Barny is actually married to Rebus's ex-girlfriend, who he falls in love with all over again.

Jim Margolies, Rebus's friend, the man who has

everything, commits suicide and Rebus suspects foul play even though Jim's father wants everything left alone.

Gill Templer admits to organising the safe house for Darren Rough, because she needed him as a witness in one of her cases. She had warned off Margolies, who was responsible for putting the paedophile away in the first place, but Rebus knew nothing of it.

After interviewing two child prostitutes and Darren himself, Rebus finds that Margolies was hiding a sinister secret, something his wife even knew about and his father had orchestrated.

Rebus helps his ex-girlfriend in finding her son. He is living with his gay lover. Barny Mee won't thank Rebus though, as Janice admits to spending the night with Rebus. It seems that Rebus has broken up the marriage.

CAST

DI John Rebus John Hannah, *DCI Gill Templer* Sara Stewart, *DCS Wilson* Ron Donachie, *DS Siobhan Clarke* Gayanne Potter, *Janice Mee* Michelle Fairley, *Barry Mee* Paul Cunningham, *Darren Rough* Russell Barr, *DI Jim Margolies* Mark Bonnar, *Katherine Margolies* Emma Currie, *Dr Joe Margolies* Hugh Ross, *Betty Margolies* Anna Hepburn, *Mary Margolies* Danielle Cook, *Stuart Mee* Iain Robertson, *Cameron Petrie* Stuart Wilkinson, *Ama Petrie* Carol Preston, *Weasel* Andrew Barr, *Van Brady* Myra McFadyen, *Ray Heggie* Paul Malcolm, *Billy Boy Brady* Ryan McIntyre, *Gordon Ince* Peter Kelly, *Kenny Lynch* Malcolm Shields, *Mrs Playfair* Pamela Kelly, *Fern* Dorothy Jane Stewart, *Francine* Stephanie Wilson, *Leanne* Kayleigh Johnstone, *Joey* Thomas Mullins,

Pete James Mackenzie, *Bouncer* Dirk Robertson, *PC* David Tarkenter, *Man Walking Dog* Colin Brown.

Standby Props John Booth, Bob Orr, *Props Driver* Andy Neilson, *Dressing Props* John Casey, Piero Jamieson, *Prop Master* Bill Gower, *Standby Carpenter* Ian Gallacher, *Standby Painter* John Hughes, *Standby Rigger* Billy Wilson, *Construction Painter* Henry Gallacher, *Construction Manager* Malcolm Gilbert, *Art Department Runner* Sarah Cowlishaw, *Production Buyer* Craig Menzies, *Art Directors* Nicki McCallom, Catherine Carruthers, *Electricians* Mick Lay, Rob Osborne, *Genny Operator* Mike Cooper, *Best Boy* Dave Cook, *Lighting Gaffer* Steve Philips, *Third Assistant Director* Emmet Cahill, *Second Assistant Director* Dee Hellier, *Script Supervisor* Sheila Johnston, *Production Secretary* Anne O'Neill, *Production Co-ordinator* Joanne O'Sullivan, *Assistant Accountant* Catrina Luna, *Production Accountant* Wim de Greef, *Location Runner* Fraser Tolmie, *Unit Manager* Miglet Crichton, *Assistant Film Editor* Laura Gorman, *Dubbing Mixer* Cy Jack, *Sound Design* Savalas, *Post Production Supervisor* Liz Pearson, *Stunts* Tony Van Silva, Peter Pocock, Vincent Kerane, Gordon Seed, *Stunt Co-ordinator* Roderick P. Woodruff, *Special Effects Supervisor* Peter Akass, *Armourer* Gregg Pearson, *Assistant Costume Designers* Rob Wooley, Christof Roche-Gordon, *Assistant Make-up Designer* Fiona Maynard, *Boom Operator* Bradley Kendrick, *Sound Recordist* Brian Milliken, *2nd Focus Puller* Kevin O'Brien, *2nd Camera Operator* Jim Peters, *Steadicam Operator* Alastair Rae, *Clapper Loader* Stephen Warner, *Focus Puller* Jason Olive, *Grip* Terry Pate, *Camera Operator* Andrew McDonnell, *Location Manager* Brian Kaczynski,

First Assistant Director Nael Abbas, *Casting Director* Di Carling CDG, *Script Editor* Nicole Cauverien, *Costume Designer* Delphine Roche-Gordon, *Make-up Designer* Alison Davies, *Music* David Ferguson, *Editor* Chris Buckland, *Director of Photography* Eric Gillespie, *Production Designer* Campbell Gordon, *Line Production* Don Bell, *Executive Producer* Judy Couniham, John Hannah, *Screenplay* Stuart Hepburn, *Producer* Murray Ferguson, *Director* Maurice Phillips.

Mortal Causes

A very good narration begins the episode concerning the two sides of Edinburgh. Then an IRA six-pack-style murder is committed under the streets of the city and Rebus is called in.

The story follows on from the last one as Janice Mee now has her own flat and starts to rebuild her life. Throughout the episode there are tensions between Janice and Rebus but they find some common ground towards the end.

Rebus finds that the murdered man is Brian Cunningham, 'Big Ger' Cafferty's son. Here the story harks back to the previous episode *The Hanging Garden*, where 'Big Ger' helped to find the person who knocked down and nearly killed Rebus's daughter. Now Cafferty, still in prison, wants Rebus to return the favour. Rebus has regrets.

A hoard of guns is found and racial tension builds. Rebus finds a group called The White Thistle who wish to exterminate any non-white Scots.

'Big Ger' is sprung from prison and Rebus finds himself repaying the debt he owes him.

Trivia: the list of White Thistle recruits Siobhan finds on Brian's computer account is the names of the production crew who worked on the Rebus series.

CAST

DI John Rebus John Hannah, *DCI Gill Templer* Sara Stewart, *DS Siobhan Clarke* Gayanne Potter, *DI Martin Kilpatrick* Michael Nardone, *Janice Mee* Michelle Fairley, *Morris Gerald Cafferty* James Cosmo, *Frankie Bothwell* Kevin McMonagle, *Mhairi Henderson* Ashley Jensen, *Caro Rattray* Michelle Gomez, *David Soutar* Paul Doonan, *Jamesie McMurray* Craig Moncur, *DS Ken Smylie* Eric Barlow, *DS Calum Smylie* Gregor Duncan, *Jools Docherty* Jenny Patterson, *Lachlan Murdock* Russell Anderson, *Teresa Cunningham* Sheila Grier, *Weasel* Andrew Barr, *Clyde Moncur* Vincent Marzello, *Eleanor Moncur* Barbara Barnes, *Dr Curt* James Bryce, *WPC Ellen Logan* Jenny Ryan, *Nahid* Surinder Hoonjan, *Christo* Mark O'Hare, *Minister* John Comerford, *Brian Cunningham* Alan Berkley, *Estate Agent* Suzanne Dance.

Standby Props John Booth, Bob Orr, *Props Driver* Andy Neilson, *Dressing Props* John Casey, Piero Jamieson, *Prop Master* Bill Gower, *Standby Carpenter* Ian Gallacher, *Standby Painter* John Hughes, *Standby Rigger* Billy Wilson, *Construction Painter* Henry Gallacher, *Construction Manager* Malcolm Gilbert, *Art Department Runner* Sarah Cowlishaw, *Production Buyer* Craig Menzies, *Art Directors* Nicki McCallum, Catherine Carruthers, *Electricians* Mick Lay, Rob Osborne, *Genny Operator* Mike Cooper, *Best Boy* Dave Cook, *Lighting Gaffer* Steven Philips, *Floor Runner* Mark McGhee, *Third Assistant Director* Emmet Cahill, *Second*

Assistant Director Dee Hellier, *Script Supervisor* Sheila Johnston, *Production Secretary* Anne O'Neill, *Production Co-ordinator* Joanne O'Sullivan, *Assistant Accountant* Catrina Luna, *Production Accountant* Wim de Greef, *Location Runner* Fraser Tolmie, *Unit Manager* Miglet Crichton, *Assistant Film Editor* Laura Gorman, *Dubbing Mixer* Cy Jack, *Sound Editor* Douglas MacDougall, *Post Production Supervisor* Liz Pearson, *Stunts* Richard Bradshaw, Stuart Clarke, Dave Anders, Gary Connery, Seón Rogers, Derek Lea, Clive Curtis, *Stunt Co-ordinator* Wayne Michaels, *Special Effects Supervisor* Mark Holt, *Armourer* Greg Pearson, *Assistant Costume Designer* Rob Wooley, Christof Roche-Gordon, *Assistant Make-up Designer* Fiona Maynard, *Boom Operator* Bradley Kendrick, *Sound Recordist* Brian Milliken, *2nd Focus Puller* Kevin O'Brien, *2nd Camera Clapper Loader* Stephen Warner, *Focus Puller* Jason Olive, *Grip* Terry Pate, *Camera Operator* Andrew McDonnell, *Location Manager* Brian Kaczynski, *First Assistant Director* Marcus Catlin, *Casting Director* Di Carling CDG, *Script Editor* Nicole Cauverien, *Costume Designer* Delphine Roche-Gordon, *Make-up Designer* Alison Davies, *Music* David Ferguson, *Editor* Chris Buckland, *Director of Photography* Eric Gillespie, *Production Designer* Campbell Gordon, *Line Producer* Don Bell, *Executive Producers* Judy Counihan, John Hannah, *Screenplay* Mark Greig, *Producer* Murray Ferguson, *Director* David Moore.

Series one summary

Although John Hannah may be a little too young to be the Rebus of Rankin's books (at the time of making the series), he is extremely credible in the role, as is the supporting cast. If one accepts that the stories are simplified for dramatic effect and some characters behave differently from the books, the first Rebus series was both atmospheric and entertaining, leaving the audience thirsting for more. Because of topical news stories, the last episode wasn't screened originally, which is a shame as several ongoing themes find closure in the last episode, making the series quite rounded.

The Falls

What is interesting about *The Falls* is that Siobhan is apparently a new acquaintance of Rebus. This is where Claire Price comes into her own and wins the viewers over despite the brevity of the script. Siobhan is amazed by Rebus's ways. This is similar to the Siobhan in the novel. Rebus works in the red, never within the constraints of the conventional side of the Police Force. Siobhan doesn't partake or pass judgment, she observes, noting the results Rebus gets. A mutual respect starts to build on the screen. However, she isn't endeared to him when she gets a flat and can't drive him to the Oxford Bar for a last-chance-saloon date with an estranged girlfriend.

The Falls is mid-evening fodder but not a patch on the book.

CAST

DI John Rebus Ken Stott, *DS Siobhan Clarke* Claire Price, *Gill Templer* Jennifer Black, *Mr Mayes* Tony Donaldson, *Philippa Balfour* Natalie Dormer, *Fiona Kollross* Andrea Hart, *Sir James Hogarth* Richard Johnson, *Forensic Officer* James McAnerney, *Miss Currie* Eileen McCallum, *David Costello* William Ruane,

Jessica Hogarth Elayne Sharling, *Miranda Masterson* Sharon Small, *Policeman* Gavin Jon Wright.

   Casting Director John Hubbard, Dan Hubbard, *Casting Associate* Kelly Valentine Hendry, *Stunt Co-ordinator* Denis Ryan, *Stunt Doubles* Nic Goodey, Lucy Allen, *Fight Arranger* Raymond Short, *Utility Stand-ins* Claire McKay, Mark Davitt, *Production Accountant* Bernadette Tervit, *Production Co-ordinator* Michael Wilson, *Assistant Co-ordinator* Margaret McDonald, *Production Runner* Gayle Cleland, *Script Supervisor* Gill Humpherston, *Script Editor* Claire Russell, *Publicist* Lisa Vanoli, *Picture Publicist* Tracey Whitton, *Unit Manager* Robbie Kirkpatrick, *Location Assistant* Christopher Cameron, *2nd Assistant Director* Simon Dale, *3rd Assistant Director* Ray Kenny, *Floor Runner* Evonne O'Rourke, *Minibus Driver* Jamie Campbell, *Unit Drivers* Jas Brown, Dugald Anderson, Edward Carey, Euan Milne, Robert Burns, *Action Vehicle Arrangers* Kristian Holt, Jack Moran, *Wardrobe Supervisor* Susie Will, Kathryn Donaldson, *Costume Assistants* Joanne Leary, Lindsey Davidson, *Make-up Artist* Laura Hill, *Make-up Assistant* Alexis McDougall, *Boom Operator* Fiona Carlin, *Sound Maintenance Engineer* Fraser McFadyen, *Art Director* Mags Horspool, *Prop Buyer* Sue Morrison, *Standby Art Director* Fiona Gavin, *Graphic Artist* Frances Connell, *Art Dept Runner* Zoe Wight, *Petty Cash Buyers* David Sneddon, Christine Gibson, *Prop Master* Piero Jamieson, *Dressing Props* Stewart Cunningham, David Weatherstone, *Props Driver* Roddy Garden, *Standby Props* John Knight, *Standby Rigger/Carpenter* Peter Callaghan, Richard Hassall, *Construction Manager* Ross Balfour, *Construction Department* Muir Balfour, David Richmond, John Smith, Bert Ross,

James Shovlin, Jane Harvey, Alex Borthwick, Julie Kirsop, James Haley, *Steadycam Operators* John Taylor, Roger Tooley, *Focus Puller* Julie Bills, *Grip* Iain Johnstone, *Clapper Loader* Julie Robinson, *Camera Trainee* Peter Keith, *Stills Photographer* Graeme Hunter, *Gaffer Electrician* Steve Costello, *Best Boy* David Moore, *Electricians* Grant McLean, David Wilson, *Post Production Supervisor* Lynn Morrison, *Assistant Film Editor* David Frew, *Colourist* Kevin Horsewood, *Dubbing Mixer* Cy Jack, *Dubbing Editor* Claire Laing, *Production Sound Mixer* Stuart Bruce, *1st Assistant Director* Patrick Conroy, *Location Manager* Michael Higson, *Costume Designer* Gill Horn, *Make-up Designer* Irene Hapier, *Production Manager* Claire Hughes, *Composer* Simon Rogers, *Film Editor* Chris Buckland, *Production Designer* Andy Harris, *Director of Photography* Alasdair Walker, *Executive Producer* Eric Coulter, *Script* Daniel Boyle, *Producer* Alan J Wands, *Director* Matthew Evans.

Fleshmarket Close

Stott is a fine actor but perhaps not tall enough to be the perfect Rebus (not unlike Jeremy Brett and Sherlock Holmes). Couple that with much shorter episodes and therefore even greater disregard to the novels, and the series was not going to win huge acclaim. Rankin fans would always be glass half empty when it came to the TV Rebus, because the novels were so intricate and the script writers just couldn't win.

Fleshmarket Close proved that Stott's incarnation of Rebus would be more gritty than Hannah's but lacked the artistry of the original series. We could forgive the complete oil theme of *Black and Blue* going missing because of the concentration/adaption of the major sub-plot featuring Bible John as the basis of the script; with *Fleshmarket Close* it was all unforgiveable.

CAST

DI John Rebus Ken Stott, *DS Siobhan Clarke* Claire Price, *Banehall Policeman* Ross Allan, *Jack Hines* Russell Anderson, *Trudy Laing* Cora Bissett, *Gill Templer* Jennifer Black, *Maisie* June Brogan, *Bunny* Tony Close, *Jim Considine* Mark Cox, *Sally Williams* Kate Donnelly, *Muzaffer Yurgi* Emilio Doorgasingh, *Merlinda Kelmendi* Aida Dumani, *Sunburst* Dolina McLennan, *Si Mc Leese* Stephen McCole, *Sabri Demir* Tahar Olabi, *Barber* Gary Stewart, *PC Ian Henderson* Anthony Strachan.

Casting Director John Hubbard, Dan Hubbard, *Casting Associate* Kelly Valentine Hendry, *Stunt Co-ordinator* Denis Ryan, *Stunt Doubles* Dominic Preece, Lyndal Smith, Brian Nickels, *Fight Arranger* Carter Ferguson, *Production Accountant* Bernadette Tervit, *Production Co-ordinator* Michael Wilson, *Assistant Co-ordinator* Margaret McDonald, *Production Runner* Gayle Cleland, *Script Supervisor* Gill Humpherston, *Script Editor* Claire Russell, *Utility Stand-ins* Claire McKay, Mark Davitt, *Unit Manager* Robbie Kirkpatrick, *Location Assistant* Christopher Cameron, *2nd Assistant Director* Simon Dale, *3rd Assistant Director* Ray Kenny, *Floor Runner* Evonne O'Rourke, *Publicist* Lisa Vanoli, *Picture Publicity* Tracey Whitton, *Dog Handler* Ian Crossan, *Unit Drivers* Jas Brown, Dugald Anderson, Edward Carey, Euan Milne, Robert Burns, *Action Vehicle Arrangers* Kristian

Holt, Jack Moran, *Wardrobe Supervisors* Susie Will, Kathryn Donaldson, *Costume Assistant* Joanne Leary, Lindsey Davidson, Joyce Kayes, *Make-up Artist* Laura Hill, *Make-up Assistant* Alexis McDougall, *Boom Operator* Fiona Carlin, *Sound Maintenance Engineer* Fraser McFadyen, *Art Director* Mags Horspool, *Prop Buyer* Sue Morrison, *Standby Art Director* Fiona Gavin, *Graphic Artist* Frances Connell, *Art Dept Runner* Zoe Wight, *Petty Cash* David Sneddon, *Prop Master* Piero Jamieson, *Dressing Props* Stewart Cunningham, David Wetherstone, *Prop Driver* Roddy Garden, *Standby Props* John Knight, Tony Sheridan, *Standby Rigger/Carpenter* Peter Callagham, Richard Hassall, *Construction Manager* Ross Balfour, *Construction Department* Muir Balfour, David Richmond, John Smith, Bert Ross, James Shovlin, *Focus Puller* Julie Bills, *Grip* Iain Johnstone, *Clapper Loader* Julie Robinson, *Camera Trainee* Peter Keith, *Stills Photographer* Graeme Hunter, *Gaffer Electrician* Steve Costello, *Best Boy* David Moore, *Electricians* Grant McLean, David Wilson, *Post Production Supervisor* Lynn Morrison, *Assistant Film Editor* David Frew, *Colourist* Kevin Horsewood, *Dubbing Mixer* Cy Jack, *Dubbing Editor* Amanda McGoldrick, *Production Sound Mixer* Stuart Bruce, *1st Assistant Director* Patrick Conroy, *Location Manager* Michael Higson, *Costume Designer* Gill Horn, *Make-up Designer* Irene Napier, *Production Manager* Claire Hughes, *Composer* Simon Rogers, *Film Editor* Chris Buckland, *Production Designer* Andy Harris, *Director of Photography* Alasdair Walker, *Executive Producer* Eric Coulter, *Script* Daniel Boyle, *Producer* Alan J Wands, *Director* Matthew Evans.

The Black Book

'You need stability in your life, you just won't allow it to happen,' says Siobhan Clarke to Rebus and she's right. Rebus starts the episode trying to apologise to his latest flame and failing miserably. He then takes his anger out on – what turns out to be – a colleague's car.

This is an episode where Rebus is at his maverick best: angry, prejudiced and totally hysterical. Rebus receives a notebook full of ciphers, which could have clues connected to a hillside murder and an almost identical unsolved murder from Rebus's past. With heart firmly on sleeve, Rebus stirs up enough trouble to solve the case through sheer force of will.

There is no burned out hotel, no Heartbreak Cafe, no Cafferty, no return of Rebus's brother; just a story lost in the ghetto.

CAST

DI John Rebus Ken Stott, *DS Siobhan Clarke* Claire Price, *DI Dalcastle* Robert Cavanah, *DCS Gill Templer* Jennifer Black, *Daniel Raeburn* David Robb, *Andy* Bryan Lowe, *Belinda* Lynsey Baxter, *Juliet Raeburn* Sarah Collier, *Colin Morton* Ian Grieve, *Martin Cowan* Stuart McQuarrie, *Eddie Raeburn* John Bett, *Sophie Raeburn* Rowena Cooper, *Joseph Cowan* James Grant.

Production Accountant Bernadette Tervit, *Production Co-ordinator* Michael Wilson, *Assistant Co-ordinator* Anna McPherson, *Production Runner* Joanna Matthews, *Script Supervisor* Margaret Graham, *Script Editor* Denise Paul, *Unit Manager* David Hancock, *Unit Manager/Location Scout*

Robbie Kirkpatrick, *Location Assistant* Christopher Cameron, *2nd Assistant Director* Alison Goring, *3rd Assistant Director* Marisa Carrara, *Floor Runner* Robin Haig, *Minibus Driver / Runner* Claire Hewitt, *Costume Supervisor* Louise Allen, *Wardrobe Manager* Joyce Kayes, *Costume Assistant* Kathryn Tart, *Costume Trainee* Helen Barron, *Make-up Artists* Mairi Morrison and Anita Anderson, *Art Director* Mags Horspool, *Prop Buyer* Sue Morrison, *Standby Art Director* Rhian Nicholas, *Graphic Artist* Frances Connell, *Art Dept Runners* Allan Ballany and Halla Groves-Raines, *Petty Cash Buyer* Christine Gibson, *Action Vehicle Arranger* Lee Farrell, *Prop Master* Piero Jamieson, *Dressing Props* Stewart Cunningham, David Weatherstone and Roddy Garden, *Standby Props* John Knight and Iain Gower, *Construction Manager* Phil Bowen, *Standby Rigger / Carpenter* John Rhymer, Richard Hassall, *Construction Department* Alexander Borthwick, Alex Robertson, James Shovlin and Max Davidson, *Unit Advisors* Jas Brown, Euan Milne and Robert Burns, *Police Advisor* Willie Manson, *Fight Arranger* James Fleming, *Special Effects* Nick Rideout, *HAL Operator* Garry Harper, *DS Nitris* Robert Scott, *Focus Puller* Julie Bills, *Grip* Iain Johnstone, *Camera Trainee* Peter Keith, *Gaffer Electrician* Steve Costello, *Best Boy* Grant McLean, *Electricians* Ross Grainger and Callum Milne, *Boom Operator* Peter Murphy, *Sound Trainees* Deborah Baillie and Alex Hay, *Publicist* Lisa Vanoli, *Picture Publicist* Tracey Whitton, *Stills Photographer* Graeme Hunter, *Post Production Supervisor* Lynn Morrison, *Assistant Film Editor* Carol MacMillan, *Colourist* Kevin Horsewood, *Dubbing Mixer* Cy Jack, *Dubbing Editors* Lorraine Keiller and Amanda

McGoldrick, *Foley Artist* Donald MacLeod, *Production Sound Mixer* Stuart Bruce, *1st Assistant Directors* David Brown, Harry Boyd and Lee Rooney, *Location Manager* Michael Higson, *Costume Designer* Gill Horn, *Make-up Designer* Ann McEwan, *Production Manager* Claire Hughes, *Composer* Andy Harris, *Director of Photography* Alasdair Walker, *Executive Producer* Eric Coulter, *Script* David Kane, *Producer* Alan J Wands, *Director* Roger Gartland.

A Question of Blood

There's an energy that starts this episode that makes good TV but confuses the initiated. The problem is that the script is based upon a gritty and socially aware novel and the intent of the writer doesn't come across at all. The very reason for adapting a good book to screen is to share that story with a different audience by doing it some kind of justice. There is no justification in taking the title of the book and a couple of locations and coming up with whatever you like! Stott and Price are good but the Oxford Bar scenes lack any substance and overall the story is too polite.

CAST

DI John Rebus Ken Stott, *DS Siobhan Clarke* Claire Price, *Marty Fairstone* James Cunningham, *Jez 'Peacock' Johnson* Andrew Barr, *Peacock's Solicitor* Paul di Rollo, *DCS Gill Templer* Jennifer Black, *Sergeant* John McQuiston, *Teri Cotter* Karen Gillan, *James Bell* Ciaron Kelly, *Lee Hartman* Jack Lyons, *Jack Bell* John Clyde, *Nurse* Jaclyn Tse, *Alan Renshaw* Frank Gallagher, *Kate Renshaw* Pamela Shaw, *Peacock's Heavy*

Tav MacDougall, *Jeff Curt* Robert Stewart, *T Wolf,* Mark McDonnell, *Robert Niles* Stephen Docherty, *Man-in-White* Alistair Hudson, *Receptionist* Lesley Cook, *Hotel Barkeeper* Graham Dalton, *Scuzzy Hotel Manager* Raymond Mearns.

Casting Director John Hubbard, *Casting Associate* Kelly Valentine Hendry, *Stunt Co-ordinator* Roderick P Woodruff, *Fight Arranger* James Fleming, *Utility Stand-in* Mark Davitt, *Jimmy Jib Operator* Vic Kusin, *Armourer* Mark Shelley, *Production Accountant* Bernadette Tervit, *Production Co-ordinator* Michael Wilson, *Assistant Co-ordinator* Anna McPherson, *Production Runner* Joanna Matthews, *Script Supervisor* Margaret Graham, *Script Editor* Mike Ellen, *Unit Manager* Dave Hancock, *Unit Manager / Location Scout* Robbie Kirkpatrick, *Location Assistant* Christopher Cameron, *2nd Assistant Director* Alison Goring, *3rd Assistant Director* Marrisa Carrara, *Floor Runner* Robert Haig, *Minibus Driver / Runner* Claire Hewitt, *Unit Drivers* Jas Brown, Euan Milne and Robert Burns, *Costume Supervisor* Louise Allen, *Wardrobe Manager* Joyce Kayes, *Costume Assistant* Kathryn Tart, *Costume Trainee* Helen Barron, *Make-up Artist* Mairi Morrison and Anita Anderson, *Art Director* Mags Horspool, *Props Buyer* Sue Morrison, *Standby Art Director* Rhian Nicholas, *Graphic Artist* Frances Connell, *Art Department Runner* Allan Ballany, *Petty Cash Buyer* Christine Gibson, *Action Vehicle Arranger* Lee Farrell, *Police Advisor* Willie Manson, *Prop Master* Piero Jamieson, *Dressing Props* Stewart Cunningham, David Weatherstone and Roddy Garden, *Standby Props* John Knight and Ian Gower, *Construction Manager* Phil Bowen, *Standby Rigger / Carpenter* John Rhymer and Richard Hassall, *Construction Department* Alexander Borthwick, Alex

Robertson, James Shovlin and Max Davidson, *Steadycam Operators* John Taylor and Kevin O'Brien, *Focus Puller* John Harper, *Grip* Lain Johnstone, *Clapper Loader* Chris Shaw, *Camera Trainee* Susan MacDonald, *Gaffer Electrician* Steve Costello, *Best Boy* Grant McLean, *Electricians* Ross Grainger and Callum Milne, *Boom Operator* Peter Murphy, *Sound Trainee* Deborah Baillie, *Sound Trainee* Alex Hay, *Publicist* Lisa Vanoli, *Picture Publicist* Tracey Whitton, *Stills Photographer* Graeme Hunter, *Post Production Supervisor* Lynn Morrison, *Assistant Film Editor* David Frew, *Colourist* Kevin Horsewood, *Dubbing Mixer* Cy Jack, *Dubbing Editor* Claire Laing and Amanda McGoldrick, *Hal Operator* Garry Harper, *Foley Artist* Donald MacLeod, *Production Sound Mixer* Stuart Bruce, *1st Assistant Director* Harry Boyd, *Location Manager* Michael Higson, *Costume Designer* Gill Horn, *Make-up Designer* Ann McEwan, *Production Manager* Claire Hughes, *Composer* Simon Rogers, *Film Editor* John Gow, *Production Designer* Andy Harris, *Director of Photography* Alasdair Walker, *Executive Producer* Eric Coulter, *Producer* Alan J Wands, *Writer and Director* Matthew Evans.

Strip Jack

By this time the show had firmly taken on its own parallel universe of character interpretations and storylines. Siobhan is more to the fore in this episode, which she isn't in the original story. In actual fact she wasn't even in the original story! But a strong supporting cast makes this a more enjoyable ride than some of the other misguided episodes. Most outstanding is Gary Lewis, who plays Gregor Jack. A great actor.

CAST

DI John Rebus Ken Stott, *DS Siobhan Clarke* Claire Price, *DCS Gill Templer* Jennifer Black, *Prostitute* Annette Westwood, *Gregor Jack* Gary Lewis, *Angela Jack* Emma Currie, *Jeff Curt* Robert Stewart, *Liz Jack* Leigh Biagi, *Kevin Quart* Andrew Clark, *Gail Maitland* Joanne Froggatt, *Alice* Alicia Devine, *William Class* Finlay McLean, *Vincent Hawkes* Gary Lamont, *Waitress* Jane Stabler.

Production Co-ordinator Michael Wilson, *Assistant Co-ordinator* Anna McPherson, *Production Accountant* Bernadette Trevit, *Production Runner* Joanna Matthews, *Script Supervisor* Margaret Graham, *Script Editor* Mike Ellen, *Unit Manager* David Hancock, *Unit Manager/Location Scout* Robbie Kirkpatrick, *Location Assistant* Christopher Cameron, *2nd Assistant Director* Michael Queen, *3rd Assistant Director* Marissa Carrara, *Floor Runner* Robin Haig, *Minibus Driver/Runner* Claire Hewitt, *Costume Supervisor* Louise Allen, *Wardrobe Manager* Joyce Kayes, *Costume Assistant* Kathryn Tart, *Costume Trainees* Helen Barron and Anna Robbins, *Make-up Artist* Maira Morrison and Anita Anderson, *Art Director* Mags Horspool, *Prop Buyer* Sue Morrison, *Standby Art Director* Rhian Nicholas, *Graphic Artist* Frances Connell, *Art Department Runners* Allan Ballany and Halla Groves-Raines, *Petty Cash Buyer* Christine Gibson, *Action Vehicle Arranger* Lee Farrell, *Prop Master* Piero Jamieson, *Dressing Props* Stuart Cunningham, David Weatherstone and Roddy Garden, *Standby Props* John Knight and Iain Gower, *Construction Manager* Phil Bowen, *Standby Rigger/Carpenter* John Rhymer and Richard Hassall, *Construction Department* Alexander Borthwick, Alex

Robertson, James Shovlin and Max Davidson, *Casting Director* John Hubbard, *Unit Drivers* Jas Brown, Euan Milne and Robert Burns, *Utility Stand-in* Max Davitt, *Police Advisor* Willie Manson, *DS Nitris* Robert Scott, *Jimmy Jib Operator* Alistair Hendry, *Focus Puller* Julie Bills, *Grip* Iain Johnstone, *Clapper Loader* Julia Robinson, *Camera Trainees* Peter Keith and Steve Cook, *Gaffer Electricians* Steve Costello, *Best Boys* Grant McLean and Paul Bates, *Electricians* Ross Grainger and Callum Milne, *Boom Operator* Peter Murphy, *Sound Trainees* Deborah Baillie and Alex Hay, *Publicist* Lisa Vanoli, *Picture Publicist* Tracey Whitton, *Stills Photographer* Graeme Hunter, *Post Production Supervisor* Lynn Morrison, *Assistant Film Editor* Martin Coyle, *Colourist* Kevin Horsewood, *Dubbing Mixer* Cy Jack, *Dubbing Editors* Amanda McGoldrick, Claire Laing and Lorraine Keiller, *Foley Editor* Donald McLeod, *Production Sound Mixer* Stuart Bruce, *1st Assistant Director* Harry Boyd, *Location Manager* Michael Higson, *Costume Designer* Gill Horn, *Make-up Designer* Ann McEwan, *Production Manager* Claire Hughes, *Composer* Simon Rogers, *Film Editor* John Gow, *Production Designer* Andy Harris, *Director of Photography* Alasdair Walker, *Executive Producer* Eric Coulter, *Script* Robert Murphy, *Producer* Alan J Wands, *Director* Matthew Evans.

Let It Bleed

Those with an imagination will find the basis of Rankin's original story here. Rebus moving from an all black suit to dark blue provided a taste of the Rebus/Clarke banter that has entertained the reader of the original novels. Good to see Rebus's love-life living up to its complex level of mayhem also. One of the better Stott episodes, but unlikely to draw more people to the original novels.

CAST

DI John Rebus Ken Stott, *DS Siobhan Clarke* Claire Price, *Sammy McNally* Alan Tall, *Secretary* Noreen Leighton, *Andrew Hamill* Pip Torrens, *Annie McNally* Anne Louise Ross, *Police Doctor* Emma D'Inverno, *Chemist* Fergus McCann, *DCS Gill Templer* Jennifer Black, *Elaine* Molly Innes, *Billy Spears* Billy McColl, *Gavin McManus* Sean Scanlan, *Amanda Morrison* Anna Chancellor, *Jack Gunner* Ron Donachie, *Sir Vivian Kirkwood* Roy Marsden.

Production Co-ordinator Michael Wilson, *Assistant Co-ordinator* Anna McPherson, *Production Accountant* Bernadette Trevit, *Production Runner* Joanna Matthews, *Script Supervisor* Margaret Graham, *Script Editor* Mike Ellen, *Unit Manager* David Hancock, *Unit Manager/Location Scout* Robbie Kirkpatrick, *Location Assistant* Christopher Cameron, *2nd Assistant Director* Michael Queen, *3rd Assistant Director* Marissa Carrara, *Floor Runner* Robin Haig, *Minibus Driver/Runner* Claire Hewitt, *Costume Supervisor* Louise Allen, *Wardrobe Manager* Joyce Kayes, *Costume Assistant* Kathryn Tart, *Costume Trainees* Helen Barron and Anna Robbins, *Make-up Artist* Maira Morrison and Anita Anderson, *Art Director* Mags Horspool, *Prop Buyer* Sue Morrison, *Standby Art Director* Rhian Nicholas, *Graphic Artist* Frances Connell, *Art Department Runners* Allan Ballany and Halla Groves-Raines, *Petty Cash Buyer* Christine Gibson, *Action Vehicle Arranger* Lee Farrell, *Prop Master* Piero Jamieson, *Dressing Props* Stuart Cunningham, David

Weatherstone and Roddy Garden, *Standby Props* John Knight and Iain Gower, *Construction Manager* Phil Bowen, *Standby Rigger/Carpenter* John Rhymer and Richard Hassall, *Construction Department* Alexander Borthwick, Alex Robertson, James Shovlin and Max Davidson, *Casting Director* John Hubbard, *Unit Drivers* Jas Brown, Euan Milne and Robert Burns, *Utility Stand-in* Max Davitt, *Police Advisor* Willie Manson, *DS Nitris* Robert Scott, *Jimmy Jib Operator* Alistair Hendry, *Focus Puller* Julie Bills, *Grip* Lain Johnstone, *Clapper Loader* Julia Robinson, *Camera Trainees* Peter Keith and Steve Cook, *Gaffer Electricians* Steve Costello, *Best Boys* Grant McLean and Paul Bates, *Electricians* Ross Grainger and Callum Milne, *Boom Operator* Peter Murphy, *Sound Trainees* Deborah Baillie and Alex Hay, *Publicist* Lisa Vanoli, *Picture Publicist* Tracey Whitton, *Stills Photographer* Graeme Hunter, *Post Production Supervisor* Lynn Morrison, *Assistant Film Editor* Martin Coyle, *Colourist* Kevin Horsewood, *Dubbing Mixer* Cy Jack, *Dubbing Editors* Amanda McGoldrick, Claire Laing and Lorraine Keiller, *Foley Editor* Donald McLeod, *Production Sound Mixer* Stuart Bruce, *1st Assistant Director* Harry Boyd, *Location Manager* Michael Higson, *Costume Designer* Gill Horn, *Make-up Designer* Ann McEwan, *Production Manager* Claire Hughes, *Composer* Simon Rogers, *Film Editor* John Gow, *Production Designer* Andy Harris, *Director of Photography* Alasdair Walker, *Executive Producer* Eric Coulter, *Script* David Kane, *Producer* Alan J Wands, *Director* Roger Gartland.

Resurrection Men

At the start of this episode Rebus is hell-bent on trying to get some sleep after being out on a bender. This causes him to make some rash decisions during a murder inquiry, which leads to him throwing a tantrum at Gill Templer and being sent to the 'last chance saloon' for naughty cops. A tall order for Rebus to be coaxed into being a team player, but after an amusing time at a massage parlour where he is discovered by Siobhan, Rebus begins to bounce back.

This is a story where Siobhan was given the opportunity to shine and Rebus at last told off. And it does at least that. One of the better episodes.

CAST

DI John Rebus Ken Stott, *DS Siobhan Clarke* Claire Price, *DCS Gill Templer* Jennifer Black, *Cynthia Marber* Stella Gonet, *Edward Marber* Jason Hetherington, *Charlie Guthrie* Bryan Larkin, *Jack Gunner* Ron Donachie, *Danny Kerr* Jamie Michie, *DI Frances Grey* Des McAleer, *DI Jazz McCulloch* Jon Morrison, *DCI Tennent* David Anderson, *Eva* Laura Marks, *Nolan* Dougie Sannachan, *Anderson* Allan Sawers, *News Reporter* Debi Edwards, *Carrie Ann* Laura Harvey.

Production Co-ordinator Margaret McDonald, *Assistant Co-ordinator* Brian Fraser, *Production Accountants* Bernadette Tervit and Denise Taylor, *Production Runner* Joanna Matthews, *Script Supervisor* Margaret Graham, *Script Editor* Denise Paul, *Unit Managers* Bobbie Kirkpatrick and Christopher Cameron, *2nd Assistant Director* Michael Queen, *3rd Assistant Director* Alison Wallace, *Floor Runner* Andy Gardiner, *Stand-in* Stephen Carney, *Costume Supervisor* Kathryn Tart, *Wardrobe Manager* Anna Robbins, *Costume Assistant* Alison Johnston, *Costume Trainee* Camille Moohan, *Make-up Artists* Mairi Morrison and Anita Anderson, *Art*

IAN RANKIN AND INSPECTOR REBUS

Director Mags Horspool, *Prop Buyer* Sue Morrison, *Standby Art Director* Alan Ballany, *Graphic Artist* Frances Connell, *Art Department Runner* Claire Fleming, *Petty Cash Buyer* Rebecca Armstrong, *Action Vehicle Arranger* Lee Farrell, *Prop Master* Piero Jamieson, *Dressing Props* Stewart Cunningham, David Wetherstone and Roddy Garden, *Standby Props* John Knight and Iain Gower, *Costume Manager* Ross Balfour, *Construction Department* Paul Curren, James Haley and Martin Fallon, *Standby Rigger/Carpenters* Ian Harrison and Richard Hassall, *Unit Drivers* Jas Brown, Euan Milne, Robert Burns and Eddie Curey, *Police Advisor* Willie Manson, *Fight Arranger* James Fleming, *Armourer* Mark Shelley, *Steadicam Operator* Roger Tooley, *Special Effects Supervisor* Neal Champion, *Focus Puller* Julia Robinson, *Grip* Iain Johnstone, *Clapper Loader* Peter Keith, *Camera Trainee* Steven Cook, *Gaffer Electrician* Steve Costello, *Best Boy* Grant McLean, *Electricians* Arthur Donnelly, Callum Milne, Paul Bates and Euan Epton, *Sound Maintenance Engineer* Simon Tomlinson, *Additional Camera Operator* Julie Bills, *Additional Focus Puller* John Harper, *2nd Unit Camera Operator* Kevin O'Brien, *Publicist* Lisa Vanoli and Tracey Whitton, *Stills Photographer* Graeme Hunter, *Prop Production Supervisor* Lynn Morrison, *Assistant Film Editor* Carol MacMillan, *Colourist* Kevin Horsewood, *Dubbing Mixer* Cy Jack, *Dubbing Editor* Amanda McGoldrick and Lorraine Keiller, *Foley Artist* Michael MacKinnon, *Casting Director* Kathleen Crawford, *Production Sound Mixer* Stuart Bruce, *1st Assistant Director* David Gilchrist, *Location Manager* Michael Higson, *Costume Designer* Gill Horn, *Make-up Designer* Ann McEwan, *Production Manager* Michael Wilson, *Composer* Simon Rogers, *Film Editor* Chris Buckland, *Production*

Tervit and Denise Taylor, *Production Runner* Joanna Matthews, *Script Supervisor* Margaret Graham, *Script Editor* Mike Ellen, *Unit Managers* David Hancock and Christopher Cameron, *2nd Assistant Director* Michael Queen, *3rd Assistant Director* Alison Wallace, *Floor Runner* Andy Gardiner, *Stand-in* Stephen Carney, *Costume Supervisor* Kathryn Tart, *Wardrobe Manager* Anna Robbins, *Costume Assistant* Alison Johnston, *Costume Trainee* Camille Moohan, *Make-up Artists* Mairi Morrison and Anita Anderson, *Art Director* Mags Horspool, *Prop Buyer* Sue Morrison, *Standby Art Director* Alan Ballany, *Graphic Artist* Frances Connell, *Art Department Runner* Claire Fleming, *Petty Cash Buyer* Rebecca Armstrong, *Action Vehicle Arranger* Lee Farrell, *Prop Master* Piero Jamieson, *Dressing Props* Stewart Cunningham, David Wetherstone and Roddy Garden, *Standby Props* John Knight and Iain Gower, *Costume Manager* Ross Balfour, *Construction Department* Paul Curren, James Haley and Martin Fallon, *Standby Rigger/Carpenters* John Rhymer and Richard Hassall, *Unit Drivers* Jas Brown, Euan Milne, Robert Burns and Stephen Harrop, *Police Advisor* Willie Manson, *Stunt Arranger* Paul Herasman, *Stunt Performers* Andy Wareham, Nick Hobbs, Kelly Dent and Lee Sheward, *Steadicam Operator* John Taylor, *Focus Puller* Julia Robinson, *Grip* Iain Johnstone, *Clapper Loader* Peter Keith, *Camera Trainee* Steven Cook, *Gaffer Electrician* Steve Costello, *Best Boy* Grant McLean, *Electricians* Arthur Donnelly, Callum Milne, Paul Bates and Euan Epton, *Sound Maintenance Engineer* Alastair Mason, *2nd Unit Camera Operator* Kevin O'Brien, *2nd Unit Focus Puller* Andrew M'Itwamwari, *Publicist* Lisa Vanoli and Tracey Whitton, *Stills Photographer* Graeme Hunter, *Prop Production Supervisor* Lynn

Hertog, *Duty Sergeant* Frank Gilhooley, *Squat Girl* Itxaso Mereno, *Duncan Barclay* Stewart Ennis.

Production Co-ordinator Margaret McDonald, *Assistant Co-ordinator* Brian Fraser, *Production Accountants* Bernadette Tervit and Denise Taylor, *Production Runner* Joanna Matthews, *Script Supervisor* Margaret Graham, *Script Editor* Denise Paul, *Unit Managers* David Hancock and Robbie Kirkpatrick, *2nd Assistant Director* Michael Queen, *3rd Assistant Director* Alison Wallace, *Floor Runner* Andy Gardiner, *Stand-in* Stephen Carney, *Costume Supervisor* Kathryn Tart, *Wardrobe Manager* Anna Robbins, *Costume Assistant* Alison Johnston, *Costume Trainee* Camille Moohan, *Make-up Artists* Mairi Morrison and Anita Anderson, *Art Director* Mags Horspool, *Prop Buyer* Sue Morrison, *Standby Art Director* Alan Ballany, *Graphic Artist* Frances Connell, *Art Department Runner* Claire Fleming, *Petty Cash Buyer* Rebecca Armstrong, *Action Vehicle Arranger* Lee Farrell, *Prop Master* Piero Jamieson, *Dressing Props* Stewart Cunningham, David Wetherstone and Roddy Garden, *Standby Props* John Knight and Iain Gower, *Costume Manager* Ross Balfour, *Construction Department* Paul Curren, James Haley and Martin Fallon, *Standby Rigger/Carpenters* John Rhymer and Richard Hassall, *Unit Drivers* Jas Brown, Euan Milne, Robert Burns and Stephen Harrop, *Police Advisor* Willie Manson, *Armourer* Mark Shelley, *Steadicam Operator* Roger Tooley, *Focus Puller* Julia Robinson, *Grip* Iain Johnstone, *Clapper Loader* Peter Keith, *Camera Trainee* Steven Cook, *Gaffer Electrician* Steve Costello, *Best Boy* Grant McLean, *Electricians* Arthur Donnelly, Callum Milne, Paul Bates and Euan Epton, *Sound Maintenance Engineer* Alastair Mason, *2nd Unit Camera Operator* Ossie McLean, *2nd Unit Focus Puller* John Harper,

Publicist Lisa Vanoli and Tracey Whitton, *Stills Photographer* Graeme Hunter, *Prop Production Supervisor* Lynn Morrison, *Assistant Film Editor* Laura Gorman, *Colourist* Kevin Horsewood, *Dubbing Mixer* Cy Jack, *Dubbing Editor* Amanda McGoldrick and Lorraine Keiller, *Foley Artist* Donald MacLeod, *Casting Director* Kathleen Crawford, *Production Sound Mixer* Stuart Bruce, *1st Assistant Director* David Gilchrist, *Location Manager* Michael Higson, *Costume Designer* Gill Horn, *Make-up Designer* Ann McEwan, *Production Manager* Michael Wilson, *Composer* Simon Rogers, *Film Editor* John Gow, *Production Designer* Andy Harris, *Director of Photography* Alasdair Walker, *Executive Producer* Eric Coulter, *Screenplay* David Kane, *Producer* Alan J Wands, *Director* Martyn Friend.

Knots and Crosses

If you were not familiar with the original novel then this would be entertaining television, but for those who are, it's another frustrating ride. There is no real reason why the original story had to be pulled around as much as this one was. OK, the idea that Rebus could have committed the murders is here – which was a possible outcome to the original novel – but this was really hallowed ground for true Rebus fans.

The actors took their parts well.

CAST

DI John Rebus Ken Stott, *DS Siobhan Clarke* Claire Price, *DCS Gill Templer* Jennifer Black, *Bobby Robertson* Graeme Rooney, *Margaret Robertson* Therese Bradley, *Peter Carr* Sam Heughan, *Barbara Carr* Lindy Whiteford, *Susan Carr* Jessica Graham,

IAN RANKIN AND INSPECTOR REBUS

Brian Robertson Brian McCardie, *Davis Haigh* Nicholas Farrell, *QC* Charles Willis Jeffrey, *High Court Judge* Iain Agnew, *Daniel Carr* Nick Rhys, *Dave Johnson* Chris Young, *Dave MacFarlane* Garry Sweeney, *Clive Dawson* Kevin McMonagle, *DS Trish Fuller* Susan Vidler, *Xan Zee Barman* Peter Milne, *Drug Squad Inspector* Russell Watters.

Production Co-ordinator Margaret McDonald, *Assistant Co-ordinator* Brian Fraser, *Production Accountants* Bernadette Tervit and Denise Taylor, *Production Runner* Joanna Matthews, *Script Supervisor* Margaret Graham, *Script Editor* Mike Ellen, *Unit Managers* Christopher Cameron and Robbie Kirkpatrick, *2nd Assistant Director* Michael Queen, *3rd Assistant Director* Alison Wallace, *Floor Runner* Andy Gardiner, *Stand-in* Stephen Carney, *Costume Supervisor* Kathryn Tart, *Wardrobe Managers* Anna Robbins and Alison Johnston, *Costume Assistant* Camille Moohan, *Costume Trainee* Ruth Webster, *Make-up Artists* Mairi Morrison and Anita Anderson, *Art Director* Mags Horspool, *Prop Buyer* Sue Morrison, *Standby Art Director* Alan Ballany, *Graphic Artist* Frances Connell, *Art Department Runner* Claire Fleming, *Petty Cash Buyer* Rebecca Armstrong, *Action Vehicle Arranger* Lee Farrell, *Prop Master* Piero Jamieson, *Dressing Props* Stewart Cunningham, David Wetherstone and Roddy Garden, *Standby Props* John Knight and Iain Gower, *Costume Manager* Ross Balfour, *Construction Department* Jane Harvie, James Haley and Martin Fullon, *Standby Rigger/Carpenters* John Rhymer and Richard Hassall, *Unit Drivers* Jas Brown, Euan Milne, Robert Burns and Stephen Harrop, *Police Advisor* Willie Manson, *Fight Arranger* David Goddall, *Armourer* Mark Shelley, *Steadicam Operator* Tony Jackson,

ANNEX C

IAN RANKIN COLLECTOR'S GUIDE

What follows is one of the most comprehensive and accurate collector's guide ever published concerning the UK first editions and their variants of Ian Rankin's work. Many of the items listed here have been studied in preparation of this guide and questions asked of Ian Rankin and his publishers as to their provenance. I would like to thank Ian and Orion for their support over the past five years, especially their time, patience and trust, which has enabled me to obtain such obscure information.

Also, Ian has been very keen to give his fans/collectors as much up-to-date information as possible with regard to the various versions of his books available. I have also spoken to him at length about very obscure issue points during our interviews in London and in Edinburgh and I would like to thank him again for his time and trouble, especially when I talked about different colour endpapers and prices on dustwrappers. He surely must have thought me mad on several occasions but managed to put up with my strange questions nonetheless!

At the 2009 Edinburgh Book Festival (specifically 19 August), Rankin was asked if there was a bibliography of his works that fans could use for reference. This became further inspiration – if inspiration were needed! – for the following detailed Annex concerning his UK published works and, as an extra treat, we begin with a short interview with him about his interest in collecting books and the collectability of his own work.[lxxv]

I noticed that a dealer is selling a draft beginning – unreleased – of Exit Music. *Do you know about that?*
'It's probably something I did for a charity. How much do they want for it?'

Five hundred pounds.
'They've got to be mad, or the person who buys it is! I'll do them one for £100! Seriously, dealers bring their stuff along to my signings, or rather they get their mums to do it. It happened the other night.

'Nowadays anyone can be a dealer, what with AbeBooks and Ebay. Anyone can do it.'

---

lxxv The interviews used for this piece come from the author's interviews with Rankin on 14 January 2002, 22 September 2004, 11 August 2005, 19 and 20 August 2009.

But the seller doesn't always have the knowledge to know what they have; they may think they do.

'I know the early books sell for a lot of money. I remember seeing a copy of *The Flood* in an auction. It had a very high price on it and it was only the paperback version. There were 800 copies printed of the paperback, compared to only three or four hundred hardbacks, so I was astonished... I've got some unopened copies in their original mailing box.

'Orion called for my early works to be re-issued. First I allowed *Watchman* because I took a look through it and thought, Yes, this holds up.'

The Flood also got re-issued, the proof having a much shorter Introduction than the final hardback, I notice. In January 2005 you were quite determined that the publisher wouldn't get their hands on that book, not until after the final Rebus novel, at least. What changed your mind?

'My publisher was keen to publish and got me drunk one night at dinner. That's probably why I said I'd think about it. I didn't like that fans/completists couldn't get access to the book, and that dealers were profiting wildly from a few fans with deep pockets. I also thought it might complement *Rebus's Scotland*, sections of which refer to my childhood in Cardenden. If I'm ever hard up, expect me to change my mind on *Westwind*, too... Also I agreed to *Watchman* and *The Flood* because of the readers, not the collectors. There were people out there who just wanted to read the books and had to pay silly money to get at the early ones. I told them they're not as good, but they told me that they didn't care: I had written them and they wanted to read them, so that's where it really made more sense to me to release them.'

Why don't you like Westwind?
'It was my attempt at a big conspiracy-theory story, set partly in the USA (a country I had never visited at that time) and with lots of humour. Unfortunately, my editor of the time didn't like it, and had me make masses of changes – taking out the humour and the US setting, for example – by the end of which I felt the book had ceased to be mine. There's a cheesy photo of me on the back, looking about 16, taken when I worked on a London hi-fi magazine. I don't think I could bear to read the novel now.

'That's the problem with collecting: it's not about quality, it's about quantity. A book could be a masterpiece and sell millions and be worth 20p on the collector's market but a load of rubbish that hardly sells and there's about five copies in existence will sell for hundreds!'

You seem to be aware of how collectable your books are?
'Yes, the early books are worth a fortune nowadays. Not so much the later books because the print-runs are high, but the proof copies still reach big prices. I was talking to a dealer once at a book signing in Edinburgh, and he had bought 40 copies of *Resurrection Men*, which he wanted me to sign. I asked him what he was doing with them, and he told me that he had punters for them all over the world.'

Did it bother you that he was going to sell them on for a profit once you had signed them?

'No, why should it? He was a customer and he bought a shopping trolley full of my books. So what? It keeps him in a living!'

You seem to sympathise with the collecting market?

'I'm a collector myself. I've collected a lot of first edition hardbacks signed by the writers. And if you ask me why I did it, I couldn't tell you. I have no idea. What difference does it make if you have a signature in a book of somebody you've never met?'

It depends if you collect them or not!

'Exactly! I've got some early Ian McEwan, Martin Amis, Anthony Burgess, George MacBeth. Some of those writers are dead now. And I tell you something else: when I sign a book, I never dedicate it, because it's always worth more undedicated on the collector's market. People don't want dedicated copies [Note: Rankin has changed his position on this for his later books, *Set in Darkness* onwards, especially as people request personal dedications at book signing sessions.]

Are you only interested in collecting signed copies?

'No, they don't have to be signed copies. I love James Ellroy and Lawrence Block, Michael Connelly. It tends to be male writers I like. I don't know why – it must be a bloke-ish thing. I even like Anthony Powell, who wrote a 12-novel sequence, *A Dance to the Music of Time*. The interesting thing for me about that book was the structure. After five years and five books, he would bring in a character you vaguely remember, and the character would meet the narrator on the street and say: "Do you remember when we used to work together?" And it's that idea of people coming back into your life that fascinated me, because that is exactly what happens. Powell said that life was like a dance and that is where the title of the book came from.'

Is it because of Powell that you write series books?
'No, I didn't intend Rebus to be a series. It just kind of happened. When you are writing a series, there will be characters you created five books ago who become of use to you again, and then you've got to remember all the things important to that character. Are they afraid of flying? Do they like fish and chips? You have to keep a whole series of lives in your head.'

Have you picked up any bargains?
'I don't think I have. I remember picking up a Muriel Spark novel once thinking that it was a bargain. It was ten pounds. I was a student then, so that was a lot of money. It was *The Prime of Miss Jean Brodie*, a famous book. And I thought, Ten pounds for a first edition hardback, great! But I found out that it was a reprint and almost worthless. It's not even worth the ten pounds I paid for it ten to 15 years ago!

'I've never been good at finding a bargain, or anything like that. If I thought, Let's go and play with the stock market, I'd end up losing my shirt!'

In crime fiction the works of Agatha Christie and even the early works of Dick Francis are very collectable nowadays. Are they for you?

'No, not really. I don't like horse riding so I don't read Dick Francis. My elder sister read a lot of Agatha Christie, but I thought about the wee little English village and this little wifey coming along and solving murders and thought, 'This is outrageous!' If you saw her coming along the garden path you'd bolt the door, because if she crossed the threshold you'd be dead by Chapter Three, so that didn't make any sense to me.'

THE INSPECTOR REBUS SERIES – 1ST UK EDITIONS

Knots and Crosses (The Bodley Head, 1987), with white endpapers and £10.95 on dustwrapper.

Hide and Seek (Barrie & Jenkins, 1991), with white endpapers and £12.99 on dustwrapper.

Wolfman (Century, 1992), with white endpapers and £14.99 on dustwrapper. (Note: this title was later reprinted as **Tooth and Nail**, initially for the US market.)

Strip Jack (Orion, 1992), with white endpapers and £13.99 on dustwrapper. Note: some dustwrappers for this title do not have a price on them (limitation unknown). However, priced wrappers are not as scarce as those for *Let It Bleed*.

The Black Book (Orion, 1993), with white endpapers and £14.99 on dustwrapper.

Mortal Causes (Orion, 1994), with white endpapers and £15.99 on dustwrapper.

Let It Bleed (Orion, 1995), with white endpapers and £15.99 on dustwrapper. Note: most dustwrappers for this title do not have prices on them (limitation unknown). During research for this book the only priced jacket to be found was through Ian Rankin himself.

Let It Bleed (Chivers Press, 2001), large print edition with different dustwrapper to first UK hardback edition.

Black and Blue (Orion, 1987), with white endpapers and £16.99 on dustwrapper. Note: only 600 copies of the hardback were printed as the emphasis was put on the trade paperback sales; half of the first hardback print run had a price on inner flap of dustwrapper and is much more desirable than unpriced (and ostensibly price-clipped) dustwrapper. This was verified to the author by Orion in 2001.

The Hanging Garden (Orion, 1988), with white endpapers and £16.99 on dustwrapper.

Death Is Not The End (Orion, 1998), 'an Inspector Rebus novella – part of the Criminal Records series of novellas, edited by Otto Penzler', white endpapers with £5.99 on dustwrapper. Note: author's afterword mentions next novel *Dead Souls*.

Dead Souls (Orion, 1999), with white endpapers and £9.99 on dustwrapper.

Set in Darkness (Orion, 2000), with white endpapers and £16.99 on dustwrapper.

The Falls (Orion, 2001), with white endpapers and £16.99 on dustwrapper.

Resurrection Men (Orion, 2002), with black endpapers and £17.99 on dustwrapper.

IAN RANKIN AND INSPECTOR REBUS

A Question of Blood (Orion, 2003), with black endpapers and £17.99 on dustwrapper, early issues with Orion press release with three-tone blue sidebar down left hand side and multi-coloured invitation to book launch.

Fleshmarket Close (Orion, 2004), green endpapers, £17.99 on dustwrapper, early issues with Orion press release with three-tone blue sidebar down left hand side. Note: a signed limited edition was issued in pictorial slipcase; the most collectable issues are still shrink-wrapped and therefore mint/untouched.

The Naming of the Dead (Orion, 2006), white endpapers, £17.99 on dustwrapper, full number string including '1' on copyright page, early issues with double-sided Orion press release with colour motif header, publicity tour information (normally stapled to press release) and 'Ian Rankin at your fingertips' double-sided promotional card.

Exit Music (Orion, 2007), red endpapers, £18.99 on wrapper, full number string including '1' on copyright page, early issues with colour double-sided Orion press release (there was an edition exclusive to Waterstones, signed by Rankin with a wrap-around band 'Meet Ian Rankin – When you win a fabulous weekend for two at The Witchery Hotel Edinburgh'). Note: I have deliberately identified the most collectable version of the last three Rebus titles – the review copies.

Exit Music (Thorndike Core, 2009), large print edition, hardback with different dustwrapper to standard UK first edition.

A note regarding publicity notes: copies of books with an original copy of a publisher's publicity notes are referred to as 'Review Copies' and are – often rightly – considered to be early issues. It is an easy bet that all Ian Rankin titles published by Orion came with publicity notes and probably those published by Century and Headline too – the latter as Jack Harvey novels. However, the earlier books are harder to make judgement on and, because no publicity notes have been seen during the compilation of this guide for the early titles, they are not mentioned; but that doesn't mean they do not exist. All review copies seen are mentioned in this guide.

REBUS NOVEL ANTHOLOGIES

Rebus: The Early Years (Orion, 1999), includes *Knots and Crosses, Hide and Seek, Tooth and Nail*.

Rebus: The St Leonard's Years (Orion, 2001), includes *Strip Jack, The Black Book, Mortal Causes*.

Rebus: The Lost Years (Orion, 2003), includes *Let It Bleed, Black and Blue, The Hanging Garden*.

Capital Crimes (Orion, 2004), includes *Dead Souls, Set in Darkness, The Falls*.

THE INSPECTOR REBUS SERIES – SHORT STORY COLLECTION

A Good Hanging and other stories (Century, 1992) with white endpapers and £14.99 on dustwrapper.

Beggars Banquet (Orion, 2002), with purple endpapers and £16.99 on dustwrapper. Early issues with Orion press release with three-tone blue sidebar to left hand side. Note: the mass market paperback also included the

Rebus novella *Death Is Not The End* and is considered a '1st thus' i.e. a first issue of that particular version of the book and therefore collectable in unread condition.

The Complete Short Stories (Orion, 2005), includes previously unreleased Rebus story *Atonement*, with white endpapers and £17.99 on dustwrapper. Note: Although the book is called *The Complete Short Stories* there are some notable omissions, all of which can be found listed in their original publication later in this bibliography.

THE INSPECTOR REBUS SERIES – NON-FICTION

Rebus's Scotland: A Personal Journey (Orion, 2005), photographed by Tricia Malley and Ross Gillespie (100 copies were issued by *The Reader's Digest* with a numbered 6x8 limited edition print; very few can be found signed).

Rebus's Scotland: A Personal Journey (Orion, 2006), first paperback edition, standard p/back size with b/w photo sections throughout (completely different cover, format and presentation to first UK hardback edition), £7.99 on back cover.

THE INSPECTOR REBUS SERIES – PROOF COPIES

Hide and Seek (Barrie & Jenkins, 1991), uncorrected proof p/back, numbered of 400 copies, slightly different colour card cover to first hardback dustwrapper.

Wolfman (Century, 1992), uncorrected proof p/back.

Strip Jack (Orion, 1992), uncorrected proof p/back, numbered of 500 copies, different pictorial wrapper to first hardback edition. Note: although this was not promoted as a signed and numbered limited edition, many copies were flat-signed by Rankin under the limitation numbers and are therefore the most desirable copies.

Strip Jack (Orion, 1993), proof for p/back issue. Brown and white card covers with Orion logo on front.

A Good Hanging (Century, 1992), uncorrected proof p/back of short-story anthology.

The Black Book (Orion, 1993), uncorrected proof p/back.

Mortal Causes (Orion, 1994), uncorrected proof p/back.

Let It Bleed (Orion, 1995), uncorrected proof p/back.

Black and Blue (Orion, 1997), uncorrected proof p/back, pictorial front cover (green fingerprint with green titles on white wrapper). Note: authenticates hardback priced wrapper of £16.99 on back cover with trade paperback price also listed as £9.99.

The Hanging Garden (Orion, 1998), uncorrected proof p/back, black and white photo of Rankin on white front cover.

The Hanging Garden (Orion, 1999), standard paperback proof 'Advanced Reading copy', with blue words on white card cover.

Dead Souls (Orion, 1999), uncorrected proof p/back, black and white photo of Rankin on white front cover.

Dead Souls (Orion, 1999), standard paperback proof 'Special Book Proof' for first p/back edition, lime green cover with titles in black. Note: this special proof was released as additional promotion to first *Rebus* TV series, starring John Hannah.

Set in Darkness (Orion, 2000), uncorrected proof p/back, with same image as standard first UK edition hardback on front cover with white spine and back cover.

IAN RANKIN AND INSPECTOR REBUS

The Falls (Orion, 2001), uncorrected proof p/back, with black covers and boxed photo identical to first UK edition hardback to front cover.

Resurrection Men (Orion, 2002), uncorrected proof p/back, with black and white photo of Rankin to front cover, some copies with additional proof wrapper (clearly identified as such) similar to first UK hardback edition, save for the proof markings.

Beggars Banquet (Orion, 2002), uncorrected proof p/back, with same photo to front cover as first UK hardback edition (short story collection).

A Question of Blood (Orion, 2003), uncorrected proof p/back, with same photo to front cover as first UK hardback edition.

Fleshmarket Close (Orion, 2004), uncorrected proof p/back, with map of Fleshmarket Close to front cover.

Fleshmarket Close (Orion, 2004), uncorrected proof p/back, with same photo to front cover as first UK hardback edition.

Naming of the Dead (Orion, 2006), uncorrected proof p/back, numbered of 250 copies only and dated '18.10.06' in red on black card cover, depicting a segment of a crossword completed, which reads 'Rankin, Rebus, Is, Back'.

Naming of the Dead (Orion, 2006), standard proof p/back copy in same pictorial wrap as first hardback edition.

Naming of the Dead (Orion, 2007), proof copy of the paperback edition, black cover with 'Rebus is Back' in bold blue capital letters.

INSPECTOR REBUS TRADE PAPERBACKS

Trade paperbacks were introduced into the Inspector Rebus series from Black and Blue. *The idea was to provide an under-£10 version of the new-release hardback novel but not a mass-market paperback. All trade paperbacks have the same dimensions as the standard hardback release, i.e. bigger than normal paperbacks, and are released simultaneously with hardback releases. With the release of* Black and Blue *the trade paperback was pushed hard – as it was the first – which meant only 600 copies of the first edition hardback were released, half the run going to libraries/book clubs, thus having no price on the inner flap of dustwrapper. Copies with priced dustwrappers are worth top prices today.*

Strip Jack (Orion, 1992).
Black and Blue (Orion, 1987).
The Hanging Garden (Orion, 1988).
Dead Souls (Orion, 1999).
Set in Darkness (Orion, 2000).
The Falls (Orion, 2001).
Resurrection Men (Orion, 2002).
A Question of Blood (Orion, 2003).
Fleshmarket Close (Orion, 2004).
The Naming of the Dead (Orion, 2006).
Exit Music (Orion, 2007).

Note regarding book club issues: as a rule book club issues of Rankin's books are not of any value. However BCA released a set of books commonly known as 'pocket editions' by fans, which are numbered on the back of the dustwrapper by their place in the series. The set is of some note as they each include a special Introduction by the author, explaining his memories of writing the books, which many people find interesting. A complete set of the books up to at least *Fleshmarket Close* or *The Naming of the Dead* is worth approximately £100. Uncommon for a BCA set of books (Rankin's three Jack Harvey novels are unnumbered extras in the series).

EARLY AND SELECTED INSPECTOR REBUS SHORT STORIES

'Talk Show' in **Winter Crimes 23** (Macmillan, 1991).

'In the Frame' in **Winter's Crimes 24** (Macmillan, 1992), hardback with dustwrapper.

'Trip Trap' in **1st Culprit** (Chatto & Windus, 1992), p/back with pictorial dustwrapper.

'Well Shot' in **2nd Culprit** (Chatto & Windus, 1993), p/back with pictorial dustwrapper.

'Castle Dangerous' in **Ellery Queen Magazine**, October 1993.

'Facing the Shot' in **Midwinter Mysteries 4** (Little, Brown, 1994), edited by Hilary Hale.

'Window of Opportunity' in **Ellery Queen Magazine**, December 1995.

'Get Shortie' in **Crimewave 2** (TTA Press, 1999), p/back with gun on playing card cover.

'Acid Test' in **EDiT**, The University of Edinburgh Magazine, Issue 15, Winter 1998/99.

Note: 'Acid Test' is especially significant because it was the first Rebus to be illustrated by the photographs of Tricia Malley and Ross Gillespie. When Rankin saw the pictures, he requested that all his book jacket photos be supplied by the duo.

'Acid Test' in **Ellery Queen Magazine**, August 1999.

'Saint Nicked' in **Radio Times** two-issue serialisation (21 December 2002 – 31 January 2003 and 4 – 10 January 2003), two-part short story with colour illustrations. Sets exist with each issue flat signed by Rankin at top of story. Note: 'Saint Nicked' was first published in one volume in *The Best British Mysteries Vol. 1* (2004).

'Fieldwork' in **Ox-Tales Earth** (Profile, 2009), short-short story the first in a set of four anthologies for Oxfam (Rankin only appearing in book one). The story also appeared in *The Guardian* on Monday 6 July 2009.

THE INSPECTOR REBUS SERIES – LIMITED EDITIONS

The Hanging Garden (Scorpion Press, 1998).

Beggars Banquet (Scorpion Press, 2002).

A Question of Blood (Scorpion Press, 2003).

Fleshmarket Close (Scorpion Press, 2004).

The Naming of the Dead (Scorpion Press, 2006).

Note: Approximately 100 copies of each of the Scorpion Press books were printed in quarter leather-bound editions with 16 lettered copies as part of each individual run. The first two copies of each title went to Rankin.

Knots and Crosses (Orion, 2007), signed and numbered limited edition of 1,500 with special introduction, previously unreleased 'deleted material' and pictorial endpapers. Matchbox striker coloured spine and boards, released in slip case without dustwrapper. Note:

This 'Collectors' Edition' was also released unsigned without limitation.

THE INSPECTOR REBUS SERIES – PRESS AND PUBLISHER'S SPECIAL HARDBACK EDITIONS

A more detailed snapshot of the desirable publicity/press copies of the later Rebus books, so inserts can be appreciated more fully.

A Question of Blood (Orion, 2003), first hardback edition with black endpapers and £17.99 on dustwrapper. Includes original press release (with three-tone blue sidebar down left-hand side), multicoloured card invitation to book launch (most copies flat-signed with 'Slainte', doodles of face or noughts and crosses doodle).

Fleshmarket Close (Orion, 2004), first hardback edition with green endpapers and £17.99 on dustwrapper. Includes original press release (with three-tone blue sidebar down left-hand side), publishers' compliment slip, invitation to book launch in unaddressed white envelope, promotional double-sided pictorial postcard 'Ian Rankin at your fingertips', and some copies with additional longer promo postcard showing a photo of Rankin and map of Fleshmarket Close. Note: the most desirable copies of these early issues have book, launch invite, and Fleshmarket Close postcard all flat-signed.

The Naming of the Dead (Orion, 2006), first hardback edition with bright yellow endpapers and standard dustwrapper. Note: this issue was printed in very limited quantities by the publisher to see if yellow endpapers actually worked; with the bright blue of the dustwrapper it definitely didn't and no more copies were printed!

EARLY UNCOLLECTED SHORT STORIES

Ian Rankin's early short stories are highly collectable. A guide to the stories released in the 1980s follows

'An Afternoon' in **New Writing Scotland Volume 2** (Association for Scottish Literary Studies, 1984), p/back.

'Voyeurism' in **New Writing Scotland Volume 3** (Association for Scottish Literary Studies, 1985), p/back.

'Colony' in **New Writing Scotland Volume 4** (Association for Scottish Literary Studies, 1986), p/back.

'Scarab' in **Scottish Short Stories 1986** (Collins, 1986). Note: 'Scarab' was re-issued with author's notes and essay in **Working Words**, edited by Valerie Thornton (Hodder & Stoughton, 1995).

'Territory' in **Scottish Short Stories 1987** (Collins, 1987).

'The Wall' in **P.E.N. New Fiction Volume 2** (Quartet, 1987), edited by Allan Massie.

'My Shopping Day' in **Ellery Queen Magazine**, November 1988.

MISCELLANEOUS SHORT STORIES

'Marked for Death' in **Constable New Crimes 1** (Constable, 1992).

'Video Nasty' in **Constable New Crimes 2** (Constable, 1993).

'A Deep Hole' in **London Noir** (Serpent's Tail, 1994), edited by Maxim Jakubowski.

IAN RANKIN AND INSPECTOR REBUS

'Someone Got to Eddie' in **3rd Culprit** (Chatto & Windus, 1994).

'Adventures in Babysitting' in **No Alibi** (Ringpull, 1995).

'Natural Selection' in **Fresh Blood** (The Do Not Press, 1996), edited by Mike Ripley and Maxim Jakubowski.

'Principles in Accounts' in **The Year's 25 Finest Crime and Mystery Stories Volume 5** (Carroll & Graf, 1996).

'The Wider Scheme' in **Ellery Queen Magazine**, August 1996.

'Unknown Pleasures in **Mean Time** (Do Not Press, 1998).

'The Serpent's Back' in **Midwinter Mysteries** (Little, Brown, 1995), edited by Hilary Hale.

'Herbert in Motion' in **Perfect Criminal** (Severn House, 1996), edited by Martin Edwards.

'The Hanged Man' in **Ellery Queen Magazine**, September/October 1999.

'Tell Me Who to Kill' in **Mysterious Pleasures**, celebrating 50 years of the Crime Writers' Association (Little, Brown, 2003).

'Driven' in **Crimespotting – An Edinburgh Crime Collection** (Polygon, 2009). Hardback in dustwrapper.

'Is This a Dagger' **The Times – Saturday Review**, Saturday 18 July 2009.

OTHER NOVELS

The Flood (Polygon, 1986).

The Flood (Orion, 2005), new re-edited version in red/black dustwrapper and special Introduction by Rankin.

The Flood (Orion, 2005), uncorrected Bound Proof with black and white photo of Rankin to cover and shorter version of new Introduction.

The Flood (Ulverscroft Large Print Books), Charnwood Large Print.

Watchman (The Bodley Head, 1988).

Watchman (Orion, 2003), new re-edited version with black and white dustwrapper and special Introduction by Rankin.

Watchman (Orion, 2003), uncorrected Bound Proof, with same cover as re-issue UK hardback.

Watchman (Orion, 2003), proof of paperback edition of the UK re-issue, colour photo of author on cover, plus book title.

Westwind (Barrie & Jenkins, 1990), with white endpapers and £11.95 on dustwrapper (some copies with distributor's review label on ffep).

Westwind (Barrie & Jenkins, 1990), uncorrected proof p/back.

Doors Open (Orion, 2008), £18.99 on dustwrapper. Note: *Doors Open* was originally released in a shorter format in the **New York Times Magazine**, 15 issues from 13 May 2007 to 19 August 2007 and is mentioned here specifically because the story is slightly different.

A Cool Head (Orion, 2009), 'Quick Reads' paperback original novella, £1.99 on back cover.

The Complaints (Orion, 2009), uncorrected manuscript proof with colour publicity notes and colour card cover.

The Complaints (Orion, 2009), £18.99 on dustwrapper.

NON-INSPECTOR REBUS SERIES – LIMITED EDITIONS

Adventures in Babysitting (Scorpion Press, 1995), Both limited numbered edition and lettered edition exists (see notes on Scorpion Press edition under 'The Inspector Rebus Series – Limited Edition').

Herbert in Motion (Revolver, 1997), includes three other short stories, numbered of 250 copies in green card covers and Edinburgh Castle photograph affixed to front. 64 pages long.

Doors Open (*New York Times Magazine*, 15 issues from 13 May 2007 to 19 August 2007). This is an earlier, shortened version of the final hardback novel.

Doors Open (Scorpion Press, 2008), first 80 numbered copies/16 specially bound copies with an appreciation by Denise Mina.

GRAPHIC NOVELS

Dark Entries (Titan, 2009), advanced reading proof copy in card wrap. Note: this is essentially a DC USA review proof. However, a couple of copies were sent across to Titan for in-house purposes.

Dark Entries (Titan, 2009), with Werther Dell'Edera in colour pictorial boards (some copies shrinkwrapped).

NON-FICTION CONTRIBUTIONS

Studio Life (Pavilion, 2008), Jack Vettriano. Foreword by Ian Rankin, hardback with dustwrapper, some copies with 8x6 promotional print. Note: copies signed by Vettriano and Rankin do exist, normally signed separately at different venues.

IAN RANKIN WRITING AS JACK HARVEY

Witch Hunt (Headline, 1993).

Bleeding Hearts (Headline, 1994).

Blood Hunt (Headline, 1995).

Blood Hunt (Headline, 1995), uncorrected proof in blue covers with black border to top and bottom of cover.

The Jack Harvey Novels (Orion, 2000), omnibus edition, with complete number line on copyright page.

Witch Hunt (Chivers Press Ltd, 2002), large print edition. Important note: I have spoken to Rankin and to editors/publicity people at Hodder/Headline, and it was suggested that between 1,000 and 3,000 copies of the first UK edition Jack Harvey novels exist, which does not justify inflated prices on the collector's market – be warned.

SELECTED MISCELLANEOUS WORKS

The Scottish Novel Since the Seventies, compiled by G Wallace and R Stevenson (Edinburgh University Press, 1993), includes Rankin's essay 'The Deliberate Cunning of Muriel Spark'.

Missing Persons: A Crime Writer's Association Anthology (Constable 1998), edited by Martin Edwards, foreword by Ian Rankin.

Ian Rankin Presents Criminal Minded (Canongate, 2000), first issue p/back, Rankin provides Introduction to short stories by Andrew Vachss, Anthony Bourdain, Jon A Jackson, Douglas E Winter and Jim Sallis. Small pocket-sized edition with £1 cover price on white card pictorial wrapper.

IAN RANKIN AND INSPECTOR REBUS

Thirtieth Anniversary of the Scottish Publishers Association: A Celebration (Scottish Publishers Association, 2004), features Rankin contribution.

One City (Polygon, 2005), p/back only, written by Alexander McCall Smith, Ian Rankin and Irvine Welsh and with an Introduction by J K Rowling. Note: copies exist multi-signed by contributors.

Stranded by Val McDermid (Flambard Press, 2005), p/back short story anthology with foreword by Ian Rankin.

Rebus (specially produced for *The Scotsman* by Orion, 2007), 'Exclusive Souvenir Paperback celebrating 20 years of Inspector Rebus', with short introduction edited from *Beggars Banquet* and short stories 'Trip Trap', 'Playback' and 'The Dean Curse', plus segment (intro plus Chapter One) from *Naming of the Dead*. With pictorial card cover.

Rebus's Favourite, The Deuchars Guide to Edinburgh Pubs (Orion, 2007), p/back only, with foreword by Ian Rankin.

Poems of Robert Burns (Penguin Classics, 2008), hardback, issued without wrapper, blue pictorial boards. Poems selected by Ian Rankin with special introduction.

Dads – A Celebration of Fatherhood from Britain's Finest and Funniest (Ebury, 2008). Edited by Sarah Brown and Gill McNeil

IAN RANKIN: THE OXFORD BAR INTERVIEW

The following piece is a bit of fun cobbled together from various interviews I have undertaken with Ian Rankin in both Edinburgh and London. I've set the piece around my own rhetorical discussion concerning the possible burning of the original manuscript of Strange Case of Dr Jekyll and Mr Hyde *by Robert Louis Stevenson, a subject both Rankin and I have discussed. However, we do — more often than not — wander into talking about Stevenson's novella in a more general way every time we meet, and in connection to the Rebus novels too.*

One interview starts with me stating that we weren't going to talk about Stevenson this time and it took us less than five minutes to do so.

Stevenson was a fascinating man and one of strong interest for Rankin and myself. The fact that Rankin's first two Rebus novels have much to thank Stevenson's Strange Case of Dr Jekyll and

Mr Hyde *for, should be justification enough for the following piece of self-indulgence from us two literary enthusiasts and, of course, the accidental additional insight it gives into the background of Detective Inspector John Rebus.*

A CASE OF JEKYLL AND HYDE
with Ian Rankin

> 'You aim high, and you take longer over your work; and it will not be so successful as if you had aimed low and rushed it.'
>
> Robert Louis Stevenson in a letter to writer and critic Edmund Gosse three days before the publication of *Strange Case of Dr Jekyll and Mr Hyde*.

Pedestrians walk in hunched obscurity behind upturned coat collars and thick woollen scarves. I'm in Edinburgh's Old Town, a location quaint in the daytime, gothically uneasy at night, so I am not intending to hang around in the dark for long. I have an interesting trip across town to make: from Castlehill, down steep North Bank Street and across Princes Street Gardens, then up into the New Town, along George Street, down Castle Street and finally left into Young Street to the Oxford Bar. It's a twisting and turning, down and up walk, but at least it keeps the circulation going in the cold!

The Oxford Bar was the now famous pub of fictional Detective Inspector John Rebus, and where I was to interview his creator, one of Scotland's most famous modern-day writers, Ian Rankin. But we weren't just interested in talking about John Rebus, we wanted to discuss another subject of common interest: the writing – and *burning* – of the original manuscript of Robert Louis Stevenson's masterpiece *Strange Case of Dr Jekyll and Mr Hyde*.

The book is of interest for many different reasons. One thing we both agree on is the idea that the original manuscript was set in Edinburgh, not London (the main location in the published book). But there was something else that fascinated me: perhaps the original manuscript of Jekyll and Hyde alluded to something Stevenson himself saw, heard – *witnessed* – when he walked around Edinburgh's Old Town during his university days, or rather, nights. At that time Stevenson was known as 'the man in the velvet jacket' by certain women of the night and, to my mind, it was quite possible that the burning of the original manuscript of Jekyll and Hyde was for a more sinister reason than Louis's wife claiming that he missed his own story's allegory.

Could the original story have implicated Stevenson in a real-life murder case, which has been shrouded in secrecy since Victorian times? Hm, yes, one's imagination can easily run away with itself, so lots to talk about, and I need the level head of Ian Rankin to put me straight on such matters.

As I walk through the Edinburgh streets, a description of London from Jekyll and Hyde comes to me and I marvel at how perfect the description is of Edinburgh all these years later, *'Round the corner from the by-street there was a square of ancient, handsome houses, now for the most part decayed from their high estate, and it into flats and chambers to all sorts and conditions of men: map engravers, architects, shady lawyers, and agents of obscure enterprises.'*

I ponder the *'agents of obscure enterprise'*. As a young writer Stevenson co-wrote a play entitled *Deacon Brodie*. Brodie was a gentleman cabinet-maker by day but had a much darker side to him at night... there was certainly so much hiding in Stevenson's story.

It is suggested that Stevenson based Jekyll and Hyde upon Brodie's dual personality, perhaps a natural progression of his original play? Well I, and possibly Rankin, believe just a little more. *'One house... second from the corner, was still occupied... and at the door of this, which wore a great air of wealth and comfort, though it was now plunged in darkness except for the fan-light, Mr Utterson stopped and knocked. A well dressed elderly servant opened the door.'*

To this day, Edinburgh's Old Town is a mixture of wealth and poverty: a rickety old vinyl music shop stood derelict, while in the flat above it a large chandelier lit the room and ostensibly the street below. Maybe one of gangster 'Big Ger' Cafferty's highly paid cronies owned the flat, I muse to myself.

I cross Princes Street Gardens, glancing across at Waverley station as I do so. *'... for a moment, the fog would be quite broken up, and a haggard shaft of daylight would glance in between the swirling wreaths... which had never been extinguished or had been kindled afresh to combat this mournful reinvasion of darkness... like a district of some city in a nightmare.'*

I make my way across to the New Town. Fellow pedestrians pass, to and fro, keeping their personal affairs hidden deep inside their thick winter coats. That is Edinburgh for you, private – shy – feelings locked away; but there is nothing wrong with that. I kind of envy it.

A coldness, like the faint touch of light rain, chills my bones as I make my way across Princes Street, up into George Street and onwards to the Oxford Bar, a stone's throw away from Stevenson's former house at Heriot Row.

As I draw up '...*before the address indicated, the fog lifted a little and showed... a dingy street, a gin palace, a low French eating-house, a shop for the retail of penny numbers and two penny salads, many ragged children huddled in the doorways, and many women of many nationalities passing out, key in hand... to have a glass; and the next moment the fog settled down again upon that part, as brown as umber, and cut him off from his black surroundings. This was the home of Henry Jekyll's favourite...*'

I walk through the pub door and instantly find myself at the bar. Ian Rankin turns round and smiles. 'Hi there,' he says. We shake hands. He is a nice guy: he buys me a drink! We go through to the back room, sit down and start our conversation:

Does Edinburgh have a dual personality?' I ask.

'Yes,' Rankin begins. 'Up until the 18th century it was a very democratic city. The rich and the poor lived cheek-by-jowl in the Old Town, which is quite a narrow area. The rich folk got fed up with this and built the New Town, which at that time was separated from the Old Town by Nor' Loch, which is now Princes Street Gardens. There was a physical barrier between rich and poor and that was the beginning of the Jekyll and Hyde side of the city. It was a city that had a public face and a private vice.'

'You're attracted to the dark side of the city's past, aren't you?' I venture.

'I'm always attracted to the dark side,' Rankin says, sipping his pint of 80 shillings. 'That's the way my mind works. I love all that dark stuff about Edinburgh and I could see it in the contemporary city as well. And when I was a student I would get up and walk into the middle of town, where all the libraries and the university were, and I would see the tourist Edinburgh and then in the night I would go back to the housing scheme where I lived.

'The first couple of books in the series were about that side of Edinburgh. It was a bit like throwing a stone in a pond and watching the ripples spread. I thought that crime novels were a good way of talking about modern Scotland, so I started to talk about its industry, its politics, the bigotry – the religious divide – and each book tries to add a little piece of the jigsaw to that, as well as adding a little bit more of the jigsaw to – what is to me – the intriguing character of John Rebus.'

'So the books are as much about Edinburgh as John Rebus?'

'I started the Rebus books to try and make sense of Edinburgh and I'm still trying to make sense of it! And I can see to an outsider coming in how the city appears to be a very cold place – psychologically cold, spiritually cold. It's very hard to try and get to know people. They're very standoffish, very shy. It's a very difficult city to get inside of. There are monuments everywhere, some to great writers, which I found very stifling when I first started out, because I was always under their shadow.'

'You mean the shadow of great writers from Edinburgh's past?'

'Yes. I couldn't escape from them. When you arrive in Edinburgh, you arrive at Waverley station, named after the Scott novel. Then in Princes Street Gardens there's this massive monument and statue of Scott. You go into the Jekyll and Hyde pub: you go past the statue of Sherlock Holmes because Sir Arthur Conan Doyle was Scottish too. You've always got these guys there, looking over your shoulder. It felt to me that everything that could be written about Edinburgh had already been written. That there was nothing left to say.

'And then along came *Trainspotting*. And the importance of that novel was that it showed a wider public that there was more to Edinburgh than just the past. Suddenly Edinburgh didn't have to be all statues, monuments, all twee, tartan, shortbread and bagpipes. And instead of talking about the castle and the rest of it you could talk about the poverty and unemployment, the various schemes there were to help people – the drug problems. The things that were in the town but not in that central part of it; suddenly the wider city was noticed. So the things the tourist doesn't see when they come to Edinburgh were considered. And that's the thing about Edinburgh; it tries to hide its true nature from you. Even during the Festival you're not going to get a taste of the real city.'

'Is there one book that sums up Edinburgh?' I ask, fishing for Jekyll and Hyde.

'There isn't one book that sums up Edinburgh, no. You would probably have to read *Trainspotting, The Prime of Miss*

Jean Brodie and *The Heart of Midlothian* by Sir Walter Scott. But if you want to get inside the psychology of Edinburgh, you have to go to a book that is not set there: *Strange Case of Dr Jekyll and Mr Hyde*, which is actually set in London but is really about Edinburgh.'

Ah, yes. This is my cue. 'The skyline in Stevenson's story is the Edinburgh skyline, not the Victorian London skyline.'

'Almost the cobblestoned streets, the back streets, the Scotch mist and everything else, yes, I agree. Also Jekyll is a Scottish name. There are a lot of people in Scotland called Jekyll.'

'But what about the legend of the original manuscript of the novel being thrown on the fire by Stevenson? Do you think the original burnt story was set in Edinburgh and Fanny – Stevenson's wife – told him not to do that…'

'… because he'd never be able to go back there? Absolutely. Not that he ever did go back, of course … *Strange Case of Dr Jekyll and Mr Hyde* is the most important Scottish novel of all time. It's the one that Scottish writers keep coming back to time and time again. And the two halves of the character – Jekyll and Hyde – to me, when I live here, sum it all up. It's the haves and have-nots. On the surface it appears very gentle and historical and cultured but under the surface there are all these seething frustrations and anger.'

'That's very interesting. I've never seen it as an angry novel.'

'Yes, the darker instincts are there. And physically the novel summed up the Old Town and the New Town. The New Town was built for all the rich people to live, because the Old Town was where all the poor people lived. So physically and psychologically, you have it all there. And it still existed in the 1980s when I wrote the first Rebus book. I actually thought that I would re-write Jekyll and Hyde as a cop novel, which is what I did with *Knots and Crosses*. And nobody got it. Nobody understood what I was trying to do. So I re-wrote the book again and that became *Hide and Seek*, the second Rebus novel. I used 'Hide' in the title and quoted from Stevenson's book throughout but still nobody got it! My Rebus books have always been about me trying to make sense of Edinburgh and the first two books was the beginning of that through the most significant book about the city.'

'I did notice that you used many of the same surnames from Jekyll and Hyde in *Hide and Seek*, such as Poole, Enfield, Carew, Edward and Hyde, oh yes, and Utterson. I can appreciate the depth of the influence.' (I also noted that the model made of the Wolfman (the serial killer) in *Tooth and Nail* was not dissimilar to the ape-like Hyde of actor Fredric March (*Dr Jekyll and Mr Hyde*, 1932) and the Hyde depicted in the famous 1930s Bodley Head illustrated edition of *Jekyll and Hyde*; so maybe another Jekyll and Hyde influence there for Rankin, albeit in a film-related sense...)

A famous quote from Stevenson's novel come to my mind: *"If he be Mr Hyde,"* he had thought, *"I shall be Mr Seek."'* Surely this was Rebus searching for the child-killer that hid in shadows? Yes, the killer is playing hide and seek. A children's game and, apparently, one of Stevenson's youth-time favourites. It was therefore intriguing to seek the devilish Mr Hyde within Stevenson's story. There was something covert, something that truly hid inside the story, something that Louis wanted to exorcise. His wife was afraid of this exorcism, hence the explanation of the burning of the original manuscript! But wait a moment, weren't important papers – letters – burnt towards the end of *Jekyll and Hyde*? *'On the hearth there lay a pile of grey ashes, as though many papers had been burned.'* Was this an admission, by Stevenson, of the burning of the original manuscript?

'Fanny didn't like the original version,' Rankin says. 'She maybe found it too grotesque, or too melodramatic. Did he burn it? I'd like to think he hid it, and it's waiting to be found. But he was in such a state, he probably did set fire to it.'

I don't think that Rankin is reading as much between the lines as I am, but there are secrets about Jekyll and Hyde that we could never expose; just like Edinburgh itself.

Rankin broke through my thought processes. 'You see, when Rebus was young he would have been told about Deacon Brodie. He was one of the main influences of the novel. Brodie by day was a member of the establishment but at night was a robber and mugger and was eventually hanged on a gibbet that he had helped to make because he was also a craftsman.

'The first couple of books in the Rebus series were exploring that side of Edinburgh. But then I took it further because I realised that the crime novel was a great way of talking about Scotland, about its politics (*Let It Bleed*), its oil industry (*Black and Blue*), its religious divide. So each book is a little bit of the wider jigsaw, as well as a further exploration into this intriguing character that is John Rebus.'

'You mention that your first two Rebus books were about the Jekyll and Hyde aspects of Edinburgh, but were they also about the Jekyll and Hyde aspects of Rebus?'

'Rebus was 40 years old in the first book and I had to give him a past. He had been married, with a kid and also he had been very close to someone else in the past. It was a Jekyll and Hyde type of thing, because the Hyde character was a person who was almost like a brother to him, but he – Hyde – grew up to hate Rebus and try to kill him.'

'So the whole of the first book was very consciously based upon Jekyll and Hyde?'

'Yes. The other important aspect there was, was the fact that Rebus had been part of the SAS, and part of the training for that was psychological warfare, and it used to be very traumatic. So Rebus and this Hyde character were wrapped up in that: they had gone through that training together – and that's where Hyde begins to think that he had been sold out by Rebus and tries to kill him.'

'It's interesting that you read so much into *Jekyll and Hyde*. What is the real pull for you with that story?'

'It's not just *Jekyll and Hyde* – I love some of Stevenson's other novels, such as *The Master of Ballantrae* and *The Weir of Hermiston*, all the dark stuff really. But there's something about *Jekyll and Hyde*: it's such a simple story in a way and yet it is this transformational story that people still relate to. Everybody has a dark side to them and that's interesting, and to take that further to look into criminals and how they are made is the next step, so there is so much within the story.'

'But do you believe the story of the burning of the original manuscript, or as you suggest, maybe he didn't burn it at all?'

'Either is a nice story – a great story – to believe, but there are other great stories based around Jekyll and Hyde. I love the story that when he was a kid he [Stevenson] had a piece of furniture in his bedroom actually made by Deacon Brodie and the nurse would tell him the story of Deacon Brodie over and again as a bedtime story. No wonder he turned out with a warped and twisted imagination!

'Stevenson had always suffered from nightmares. They began as a child growing up in Heriot Row, which is two streets away from where we are right now! One of Stevenson's nightmare dreams as a child concerned a real-life wizard Major Tom Weir. A respectable preacher, Weir shocked his parishioners by confiding that he practised bestiality and incest. Weir and his sister Jean were sentenced to be strangled and burned at the stake in 1670, and Stevenson's nanny "Cummy" used to scare him with spooky tales of Weir!'

When I analyse the Jekyll and Hyde story I find some interesting things. The first is the amount of wine consumed or, at least poured, for the various characters! There are many references made to wine consumption, drinking in excess, such as a drunk who *'reasons with himself upon his vice…'* But the inner secret about Jekyll and Hyde wasn't about alcohol, was it?

'*I began to be tortured with throes and longings, as of Hyde struggling after freedom; and at last, in an hour of moral weakness, I once again... swallowed the transforming draught.*' If we replace 'draught' with 'drug' and then view the '*tortured... throes of longing*' as a form of cold turkey, we may well be unlocking a very sinister chapter within the story and, quite possibly, its author's life!

Dr Henry Jekyll becomes addicted to his own drug. When he first takes it he describes the extreme sensations of the transformation into Mr Hyde as something not so unpleasant as what may be initially thought: '*There was something in my sensation, something indescribably new, and, from its novelty, incredibly sweet.*'

Any drug has this effect to begin with and Jekyll admits to the beginning of his folly: '*... It was an ordinary secret summer that I at last fell before the assaults of temptation.*'

Could this indeed be the Hyde in Stevenson talking – the man in the velvet jacket? I think not. Well, not about himself anyway – perhaps an old university friend, a man who took the temptations of life a lot further than Stevenson, a man who would – like Henry Jekyll – confide his sins to an old school friend (Dr Lanyon in the book; Stevenson in real life?): '*I mean from henceforth to lead a life of extreme seclusion; you must not be surprised, nor must you doubt my friendship, if my door is often shut even to you. You must suffer me to go my own dark way. I have brought on myself a punishment and a danger that I cannot name. If I am the chief of all sinners, I am the chief of sufferers also. I could not think that this earth contained a place for suffering and terrors so unmanning; and you can do but one thing... to lighten this destiny, and that is to respect my silence.*'

Two people share – suffer – Dr Jekyll's terrible secret, and one of them dies through the knowledge of its facts. We know that Stevenson woke from a fever dream to write *Strange Case of Dr Jekyll and Mr Hyde* at pace (30,000 words in three days apparently). Was this rush a determined push to exorcise himself from a past episode in his own life, one that he now needed to confront? Did he feel guilty that he couldn't help a former friend who had fallen from grace? Who had to be *'close to… drugs'* and who committed suicide – like Henry Jekyll – as redemption for something he did under that terrible influence?

It cannot be ruled out but it cannot be proved. However, it is fascinating to speculate, isn't it? I share my thought processes with Rankin.

'I talk about Jekyll and Hyde in a BBC4 documentary and discuss the reasons why the story is set in London,' he says. 'Robert Louis Stevenson was thinking of a real doctor, John Hunter, who was a Scot. His home sat on Leicester Square. In the book Stevenson gives a description of Jekyll's home and it is identical to Hunter's. But Hunter was a dark man: he would receive corpses at the back door to examine, stuff like that.'

Every time Rankin and I meet, we love to talk about Jekyll and Hyde. What adds extra intrigue to the legacy of the novella is the fact that two years after it was written, the theatrical production was a huge hit on the London stage during the Jack the Ripper murders. The leading man was so convincing in his role, he was even suspected of being the Ripper himself! This isn't something Stevenson could have predicted, but it does allow us to muse if he knew the

Ripper's counterpart on the backstreets of Edinburgh's Old Town and changed the location to Soho, London (but sadly not London's East End) in the final novel.

Sadly, I have gone a little too far, as Rankin shakes his head sadly. 'No, there were no Ripper murders in Edinburgh – just Burke and Hare, about whom RLS wrote short fiction. Plenty of other grim stuff was happening though… I think another reason why Stevenson set the book in London is that he didn't want readers equating Jekyll with the author – RLS having explored his own "dark side" when a young man on the streets of Edinburgh. And maybe Fanny saw too much of her husband in the story and the locations got swapped because of that.'

Well, yes, maybe it was as simple as that…

> 'Nearly a year later, in the month of 18-, London was startled by a crime of singular ferocity, and rendered all the more notable by the high position of the victim. The details were few and startling.'
> Robert Louis Stevenson, *Strange Case of Dr Jekyll and Mr Hyde*

FURTHER READING AND COPYRIGHT NOTES

The works of Ian Rankin (copyright Ian Rankin) quotes used by permission of the author

Rebus's Scotland: A Personal Journey (Orion, 2005), Ian Rankin, photographed by Tricia Malley and Ross Gillespie

Kidnapped (Cassell & Co Limited, 1886), Robert Louis Stevenson

Catriona (Cassell & Co Limited, 1893), Robert Louis Stevenson

Ballads (Cassell & Co Limited, 1890), Robert Louis Stevenson

Edinburgh: Picturesque Notes (1879), Robert Louis Stevenson (Pallas Editions, 2001) used in research of this book

The Complete Short Stories (The Centenary Edition), Robert Louis Stevenson, Edited by Ian Bell, Mainstream Publishing Company (Edinburgh) Ltd in association with The Scottish Arts Council (2 vols, 1993)

The Prime of Miss Jean Brodie (Macmillan, 1961), Muriel Spark

Private Memoirs and Confessions of a Justified Sinner, James Hogg (Longman, Hurst, Rees, Orme and Green, 1824)

The Complete Sherlock Holmes, Arthur Conan Doyle (Vintage Classics, 2009) (150th Anniversary edition with an Introduction by P D James)

Poems of Robert Burns — Selected and with an Introduction by Ian Rankin (Penguin Classics, 2008)

IAN RANKIN INTERVIEWS CONDUCTED BY THE AUTHOR

February 2000, 11 November 2000, 14 January 2002, March 2002, 27 August 2003, 22 September 2004, 5 November 2004, 11 August 2005, 26 July 2009, 19 August 2009, 20 August 2009, 4 September 2009.

AUTHOR'S NOTE

Like Ian Rankin I believe in serendipity. While writing this book there were more happy coincidences than I could ever wish for, from the small – Rebus putting on the Rolling Stones' *Rock 'n' Roll Circus* (*The Hanging Garden*), which I had done several hours previously – to the large – sitting next to a Scot on a London commuter train and reading the same Rebus novel and consequently getting his perception of the series and Edinburgh and forming a friendship.

All of this would bring a smile to Rankin's face, I'm sure. The whole of the Rebus series is about serendipity, happenstance, synchronicity, coincidence, call it what you will. It's about the people that flow in and out of our humble lives and influence and shape it for better or worse (yes, exactly what the Rebus series embraces – although Rebus doesn't believe in such a thing!).

I would just like to give thanks to all the people who have provided a bit of serendipity for me in the writing of this book.

Craig Cabell
Blackheath, London
June 2009

ABOUT THE AUTHOR

Craig Cabell was a freelance journalist and writer for 20 years. He spent five years as an in-house reporter at *Focus,* the house journal of the Ministry of Defence, and has written 15 books as a biographer and historian. He is an expert on rare and collectable fiction, from Charles Dickens to Ian Rankin, and wrote several regular wine columns for different magazines as well as travelling the world, from Kuwait to Venezuela, for government services. Some of his previous books, such as *Operation Big Ben, the anti-V2 Spitfire Mission 1944-45* (with Graham A Thomas) and *Ian Fleming's Secret War*, have attracted much praise. His previous books with John Blake, *James Herbert — Devil in the Dark, Snipers* (with Richard Brown) and *Getting Away with Murder* (with Lenny Hamilton), have showcased his diversity and specialist skills in literature, small arms and true crime. He lives in London with his wife and three children.

BOOKS BY CRAIG CABELL

Frederick Forsyth — A Matter of Protocol, the Authorised Biography

The Kray Brothers — The Image Shattered

James Herbert — Devil in the Dark, the Authorised True Story

Operation Big Ben — The Anti-V2 Spitfire Missions 1944-45 (with Graham A Thomas)

VE Day — A Day to Remember (with Allan Richards)

Snipers (with Richard Brown)

Dennis Wheatley — Churchill's Storyteller

Getting Away With Murder (with Lenny Hamilton)

Witchfinder General — the Biography of Matthew Hopkins

Ian Fleming's Secret War — Author of James Bond

The History of 30 Assault Unit — Ian Fleming's Red Indians

Ian Rankin and Inspector Rebus

Captain Kidd (with Graham A Thomas and Allan Richards)

Blackbeard (with Graham A Thomas and Allan Richards)

The Doctors Who's Who

CHAP BOOKS

Dennis Wheatley and the Occult

Black Sniper (fiction)

I Was Alive Then — The Spike Milligan Interviews

The Grapes of MoD — Ten Years of Wine Consumption

30 Assault Unit User Manual

Tales of Verona

The Curse of the Baskervilles

William — A Marine's Story

Robert Heinlein — The Complete UK Bibliography and Collector's Guide

Stephen King — Illustrated UK Bibliography and Collector's Guide

Ian Rankin Illustrated UK Bibliography and Collector's Guide

A Christmas Vampire (fiction)

Why Did I Ask Them Around to Dinner? (fiction)

The Arms Dealers Arms

Stories with Wine

SPECIAL INTRODUCTIONS

Furies Over Korea — the story of the men of the Fleet Air Arm, RAF and Commonwealth who defended South Korea, 1950-1953 by Graham A Thomas

Firestorm, Typhoons Over Caen, 1944 by Graham A Thomas

Terror from the Sky — the Battle Against the Flying Bomb by Graham A Thomas

The Biography of Dan Brown by Graham A Thomas